Mountain Stories

Remembered journeys in the
Scottish Highlands and Islands

little peak press

Mountain Stories – Heather Dawe

First published in 2021 by Little Peak Press

www.littlepeak.co.uk

This book is a work of non-fiction, based on the life, experiences and recollections of Heather Dawe. In some limited cases the names of people, place, dates and sequences or the detail of events have been changed solely to protect the privacy of others. The author has stated to the publishers that, except in such minor respects not affecting the substantial accuracy of the work, the contents of the book are true.

Edited by Jo Allen

All illustrations by Heather Dawe

Design and Production by Rhiannon Hughes,
www.theyorkshirewordwright.co.uk

A CIP catalogue record for this book is available from the British Library.

ISBN: 978-1-9160812-4-6

FSC
www.fsc.org
MIX
Paper from
responsible sources
FSC® C005094

Printed and bound in the UK

This book is dedicated to Alanna
and Robyn.

Contents

Foreword

My first experience of Scotland came when I was eight. My mother had gathered up her young family and transported us by train and sea from the landlocked flatlands of Cambridgeshire to the remote Isle of Eigg in the Inner Hebrides. For two weeks I was immersed in the scents, sounds and sensations of a Scottish landscape. I ran bare-legged through bluebell woods, marvelled at the reek of wild garlic, swam in sheltered bays of crisp azure water, and searched the sky above towering cliffs for golden eagles. It was here that I climbed my first Scottish peak, An Sgùrr, a sheer nubbin of volcanic rock, only 393m tall, but it felt as serious to my young mind and body as a Himalayan summit. We spent one week staying with friends in a haunted old manse lit by gas lamps, overlooking meadows and a narrow burn that ran down to the sea where otters played. The second week it was just us – Mum, my brother and I – in a tiny wooden cottage that felt like a ship nestled on the foreshore of a lush bay scattered with yellow flag irises. It was a heady time; the intense memories we made on that trip are vivid almost forty years later.

Now I live on the Isle of Arran, slightly further south, but, like Eigg, it is a wild and lumpy island with mountains that I call home. I'm qualified as a Mountain Leader and work in the hills, leading and training others, and I write about my love of Scotland's wildness. I am embedded in this rich and vibrant landscape, but it doesn't take much to transport me back in time to that first adventure on Eigg. A splash of blue flowers amongst the green of Atlantic oaks, or the silken head of a seal emerging from dark waters, and I'm a kid again, seeing all this for the first time. As a family, when we get together and reminisce about Eigg, our memories have become preserved in family legend, and there is joy in the shared telling of them. But there is more, in retelling them here, I am adding my memories to the story of that place.

This is a book of Heather Dawe's stories. While I was preparing this foreword, each chapter dropped into my inbox like a postcard from the places I love. I quickly felt a strong connection to Heather's voice, bringing to mind my own recollections. Like me she has spent years exploring, loving and describing these magical places. In *Mountain Stories*, she shares memories that are vivid in her mind as she writes during lockdown in the middle of the coronavirus pandemic. No landscape is two-dimensional and she interweaves her stories with tales from the land and the work of renowned poets and artists, such as Nan Shepherd and Norman MacCaig, from whom she takes inspiration. Running through them all is the rhythm of the earth, the spatter of the rain, the cool of the wind and the rush of waves on the shore.

It was a thrill to read about Heather's journeys in places that I know well, and also to discover new ones that I have yet to experience. I feel that if she loves a place, I will too. Her stories are hers alone and yet there are elements that seem familiar in a confirming way, as if we've been there together. An unforgettable cloud inversion on the Kintail ridge, the delicious pain of longing for a peak that is beyond reach, or the heart in mouth feeling of descending a snowy bealach that, with hindsight, perhaps we shouldn't have. There is a gentle circularity to the stories – each one weaves personal memories while drawing in threads from the experiences of others who have loved these places too. With this comes a sense that these stories are unfinished, and we shall return to these summits and add new yarns to the telling. There is depth to each chapter, with ripples of stories that flow outwards, and time is needed to explore where these take us, to ponder their true meaning, as Heather never labours these points beyond her own quiet observations.

Heather is a runner, and usually moves very quickly through the landscape, relishing the rough, boggy terrain away from paths the best. She covers the ground faster than many of us ever will, encompassing big days as expansive as the mountains ranges she runs in, but she sees the landscape with an artist's eye, and depicts her thoughts and feelings about her mountain journeys in a way that resonates with anyone who has spent time in the hills. Her tales span life's journey, recalling a time in her youth when she accessed the high peaks with carefree confidence, and more recent times when she must fit her mountain runs between childcare and family adventures. She asks big, relevant questions, with a light touch, about belonging, connection, landscape and motherhood. Bringing her family to the Highlands and Islands brings me back full circle to my own exhilarating first steps on Scottish bog and rock. I wonder if the children she is raising will, like me, have intense memories of childhood discoveries that will draw them back to bigger and higher places when they are full grown?

This is a book about longing and belonging, about love and letting go. It's a book about one woman's drive to explore land and legend, place and people, deeply personal, but at the same time always looking outwards at the wide sweep of the horizon and intimately connected to those who have gone before. It has kindled a desire within me to return to my beloved places, and to seek out new ones. I hope that it will do the same for you.

Lucy Wallace
President, Ramblers Scotland
Isle of Arran
June 2021

Introduction

These are my stories of mountains. Every hill-goer, hill-looker or hill-knower will have their own. I used to think to love them you had to climb them, but now I think that is wrong. You don't need to climb a mountain or even look at a mountain to love it. Just to know it's there can be enough.

I chose the hills of the Scottish Highlands and Islands for these stories because I miss them. I'm writing these words in late 2020, a year ravaged by a pandemic. This will be the first year in over two decades I have not spent time among these mountains, exploring them, looking at them, feeling their grandeur and beauty. In drawing them and writing about them I use my memories to return to them. Not at all the same as being there, but reassuring nonetheless.

It was in the Scottish Highlands where I properly learned hill-craft – the ability to take care of myself in the mountains. How to navigate, to read the hills, to know when in poor conditions to retreat to the valley and wait for another day and when to keep going. I have been lost so many times, cold, hungry and tired, wishing I was somewhere else. I think you have to experience these hard times in order to truly appreciate the days of wonder – sunny days, snowy days, days when you see all the seasons and the light on the mountains is something else. These mixed-up kind of days when the light changes constantly are some of the best for painting. The sky a blend of blue, white and dark grey clouds and the sun lays its rays over different parts of the landscape, casting deep shadows in places and exploding colour in others.

Some of the hills I write of are Munros, many are not. While I have probably climbed around 200 of the 282 Munros, I am not

counting. My partner, however, does count, and over the years through mountain journeys with him, I have explored many parts of the Highlands in pursuit of their summits. That is the good thing about Munros – bagging them takes you all over the Highlands to explore the varying terrain and landscape. The reason I do not count them is because I don't want my own journeys into the Scottish hills to be reduced to a list of summits. I have enough lists in my life. Ticking off Munros can lead to tunnel vision and I want to visit places in the Highlands and Islands because of their beauty, challenge and culture, not because they have the highest peaks. Arran, the Uists, Moidart, Rhum, Ardnamurchan, Harris and many other places spring to mind. Merits measured by height alone fall short.

I love that regions of the Highlands and the Islands have their own personal character, things that differentiate them from one another. Look to the Cairngorm Plateau and the jagged peaks of Skye's Black Cuillin and this variation is clear. Assynt, the Flow Country of the Far North, the machair, bogland and smaller peaks of the Uists, the ridges of Kintail, the Rough Bounds of Knoydart. These are just a few of them. I could spend the rest of my life in any one of these places and be content. That there are so many different mountain characters so close to each other blows my mind when I stop to think about it. I feel the need to get my feelings and memories, my real and imagined journeys, down in words.

Alongside painting and sketching, writing takes me back to the mountains and reading the words of others does the same. Nan Shepherd, Sorley MacLean, Norman MacCaig, Neil Gunn and more. Writers on and of the Highlands whose own words, whether in poetry or prose, evoke the characters of the high places that they so clearly loved. There are so many mountain stories.

1. Ben Hope
The Promise of Company

Maybe it's fitting to start with one of the furthest away hills, Ben Hope. A translation of its original Gaelic *Beinn Hòb* – meaning Hill of the Bay – this mountain rises up from the boglands surrounding it – the Flow Country.

This Flow Country is a special place – likely the largest area of blanket bogland in the world. An acidic mix of peat, moss and heather that covers much of Caithness and Sutherland, the two most northern and remote regions of mainland Scotland. In low light this bogland can seem dull and unwelcoming, but with a little sun it can feel different altogether, a thousand tints of brown, yellow, ochre and gold.

The hills of these regions rise from this tundra, their ridges and folds pushing up through the flatlands, upsetters of the equilibrium as all peaks are. While Ben Hope is well known to Scottish hill-goers as the most northerly Munro, close to it are Ben Loyal, Arkle and Foinaven. These mountains are not as high, yet they look to have at least as much character – they are still mysteries to me; I have not yet stepped foot on any of them. Foinaven in particular appeals. Casting its shape in my head from looking at maps and remembering my last view of it – snow-topped with cloud blowing fast eastwards over its summit plateau set against a dark-grey sky – sets me dreaming about trips to the north.

Ben Hope is a triangular lug of a hill, sheerest on its western side, its main ridge running from its steep and highest northern end to the far lower south. Its craggy north-west face is steep enough to have noted winter climbs. The north-east face descends less steeply, but surely, down to four large lochans and then more open ground towards Ben Loyal.

With my partner Aidan, I climbed Ben Hope in the spring of 2011. Early in May, we stayed for a week near Stoer in Assynt, part of a three-week trip to the Highlands. We were lucky with the weather for the whole of those three weeks. High pressure settled over the north, giving us the conditions we'd hoped for.

This trip marked the end of one part of our lives and the beginning of another – ten months later our first daughter was born. Something we wanted and welcomed, though we would miss our freedom to roam – at least for a while. We binged on the North West Highlands. Along with Assynt and the Far North, we went into the Fisherfields, traversed the great ridges of Torridon, explored the Glen Carron hills and, finally, those of Glencoe before we headed home.

In Assynt we stayed in a small cottage close to the coastal road that runs from Lochinver through the small townships of Stoer and Drumbeg and joins the main road north underneath Quinaig, one of the striking, isolated mountains for which Assynt is so renowned. It was a short, boggy run from the back garden to the Old Man of Stoer, the sandstone sea-stack close to the Stoer Lighthouse. Early one morning I saw dolphins playing in the water close to the Old Man, skimming through the swell as it rolled and broke against the rocks at the base of the cliffs.

Stoer is a base for the Assynt Crofter's Trust. Its surrounding land is community owned by the Trust, one of the rare progressions back to local land ownership after the forced evictions of the Clearances through the 19th century. Throughout whole regions of the Highlands people were removed from their homes and land to make way for sheep farming. A crime against humanity and a ramping up of the agricultural practices that were then expanding into the industrial revolution. Here we are today, trying to cope with the climate crisis that is the outcome of such changes. In returning to local ownership and crofting – the practice of small-scale community farming and food production – the Trust has closed the circle. Reflecting the modern era, they have built and run a small hydro-electric power station on the North Assynt Estate at Loch Poll.

It was a bright, cold and clear morning in Stoer when we left to drive further north. From the front door of the cottage was the superlative sight of the hills of Assynt across the horizon. I froze five of those hills in an oil painting later that year, back home and three months pregnant, inspired by the scene that morning and the words of Norman MacCaig:

> Glaciers, grinding West, gouged out
> these valleys, rasping the brown sandstone,
> and left, on the hard rock below – the
> ruffled foreland –
> this frieze of mountains, filed
> on the blue air – Stac Polly,
> Cul Beag, Cul Mor, Suilven,
> Canisp – a frieze and
> a litany.

These lines are an extract from 'A Man In Assynt', MacCaig's most political poem, in which he is lyrical about the beauty of Assynt and critical of its history of depopulation and mismanagement by distant wealthy landowners.[1]

> Who owns this landscape? –
> The millionaire who brought it or
> the poacher staggering downhill in the early morning
> with a deer on his back?
>
> Who possesses this landscape? –
> The man who brought it or I who am possessed by it?

Ben Hope

> False questions, for
> this landscape is
> masterless
> and intractable in any terms
> that are human.

While MacCaig was certainly on the side of the crofters, the above lines question the right for anyone to own Assynt. MacCaig and his poem became emblematic for the crofters and their objective of regaining the land. He died in 1996, not living to see the community land buyout by the Trust in 2003. He will always be associated with it.

We drove towards Ben Hope, along the main road from Ullapool, over the bridge at Kylesku, past Scourie and left at the junction over the Laxford Bridge, with such fine views of Foinaven I wondered why we would not be going there.

A sea fret – what do they call them up there? – started to close down the sunshine, the mist becoming thicker as we approached the hills of the Far North. A quick stop to climb Ben Klibreck (despite preferring to avoid them, this was a Munro-bagging day) and we were back in the car to continue to the foot of Ben Hope.

From the car park at the bottom of the Allt a' Mhuiseil burn and a large sign reading 'Footpath up Ben Hope' we began to climb. Steeply for the first mile or so to gain the ridge, then a gentler climb to the summit. It was disappointing not to get a view, but aside from the mist the weather was benign – there was little wind to speak of and it had turned into a warm May day. As we climbed I quietly hoped we would pull clear of the clag, but that did not happen. We did get something approaching ethereal light at the summit; the late afternoon sun kept threatening to burn through, but never quite made it.

19

We climbed Ben Hope before the establishment of the North Coast 500, the long-distance route around the Northern Highlands that has surely been far more successful than was originally envisioned in pulling people further up the country for their holidays and road trips. It's busier up there now, at least during certain parts of the year.

As I write I'm imagining a quieter time and the landscape in the short and low light of winter. I'm climbing Ben Hope again, alone, a pack on my back contains crampons and strapped to it is an ice-axe. Although it's unlikely I'll need them today, it pays to be prepared in the Scottish hills – especially in winter. The weather is a mix of sunshine and cold sleet showers that cross the mountain in bands; one minute you have a clear view out over the Flow Country, Cape Wrath and the sea beyond, the next you're squinting to be able to see as heavy wet droplets of sleet are blown hard against your face. It feels quite oppressive but perversely it's welcome, these feelings of discomfort are part of what hill-going in Scotland is all about.

Other parts of the same experience include looking out across the surrounding flat ground from high on the hillside when the sun breaks through the cloud and lights the land, its brown heather, lochans and moss a glow of colour – mostly browns, greens and gold in there too, interspaced with the fleeting blue of the clearing sky reflected on pools of water. I imagine this light, can almost feel the sleet against my face, a stray drop blows straight into one of my ears so I pull down my buff down from the top of my head to cover them both.

Aside from the procession of camper vans, motorbikes, and the odd cyclist along the winding coast road, many cruising the North Coast 500, the land is empty. What must it have been like in the old crofting communities before the Clearances? Scattered here and there on lower ground are the remnants of stone buildings – all that's left of the ruined shielings – no roofs as the turf they were made of would have been the first part of the building to fall back into the land.

In my mind I continue to the summit of Ben Hope. The sleet has turned into the damp kind of snow that settles on the ground enough for your feet to sink into, my fell-running shoes become soaking wet. I wonder if I should stop to put on extra clothes or just keep moving fast enough to stay warm and decide on the latter.

As I approach the summit cairn the weather closes in further. I pull a waterproof cap from my pocket, fleece-lined with flaps to cover my ears, quickly putting it on as I turn into the wind to reverse my route up the hill. Lowering my head into the wind, the peak will offer my eyes some protection against the now driving snow. Finding I can lean into the gusts, I make slow but steady progress down the hill until eventually the snow recedes, becoming rain. I plod on, the studs of my shoes making the familiar tracks of a fell runner in the mud of the path.

While my imagined climbing of Ben Hope in winter sleet may seem a morose experience, it is anything but. I love the Far North and Assynt. Although I have seen them on clear, warm, sunny days, this is not how I remember them. It's the moody times I love the most in these strange isolated hills. Rarely linked by ridges, their age and geology mean they stand alone, stark shapes on the skyline, their bases brown with tundra, higher parts dusted white with snow.

Ben Hope is one of these isolated mountains. From where I'm writing it's the last and furthest hill, a pinnacle of remoteness. But what must it have meant to those approaching the sanctuary of the bay from the north, from the open sea? The fishermen and other sailors. For them it would have marked the hope found in calmer waters and the promise of company.

2. Hecla, Ben Corradail, Beinn Mor

The three peaks of South Uist

The polymath Tim Robinson was eighty-five and in ill health when he contracted coronavirus and passed away on 3rd April 2020 soon after the death of his life-partner Máiréad. Robinson spent many years of his life on the west coast of Ireland. It was here he found much of the source material for his work, which brought together art, mathematics and creative non-fiction. His maps alone are incredible things – detailed, intricate and beautiful studies of land and place.[2]

I only discovered his writing, art and maps a few years ago. In reading and looking at them, through their great insight and the thinking they generated in me, I found, and continue to find incredible inspiration. I used to believe that finding inspiration in this way is a kind of copying, something I shouldn't do, that I needed to always find my own way. Over the years I have come to realise that this is one of the most (if not *the* most) important sources of creativity. The notion of 'standing on the shoulders of giants' exists for good reason. In sharing their work, people like Robinson offer up gifts for us all to enjoy and learn from.

Robinson's *Connemara* trilogy is recognised as a masterpiece of place writing.[3] Three books that go deep into the land, life, history and culture of the many peninsulas of Connemara. His

words evoke the natural beauty of the west coast of Ireland and explore its history and science in ways that blend it all together to make something wondrous. Was it his polymathic ways that enabled him to do this? That he could see and understand many different intellectual disciplines, and bring them together with beautiful writing was his genius.

Shortly after his passing I reread *Listening to the Wind*, the first part of the Connemara trilogy. While I've spent time in Northern Ireland, around Belfast, Antrim and the Mourne Mountains, I've not visited the west of Ireland. At home in Yorkshire, a few months into a pandemic second wave and a lockdown that is becoming increasingly strict, my mind was wandering even more than usual. I am lucky to live in a place with open countryside, woodland, moor and nature close by. While I really miss the mountains, I can wait to spend time in them again. I know they have a habit of not going anywhere fast; they'll still be there when I can next get to them. All that said, over the past decade or so, I have found ways of getting to mountains and wild land other than physically. Writing about them, painting, reading about them, takes me there. I have been mining memories – my own and those of others – of places I have travelled to and spent time wandering across.

In *Connemara* Tim Robinson writes of the wonders of the boglands above and around his home in Roundstone, describing them in terms of their geology, natural history and beauty:

> There are a hundred or more lakes in the twenty-five or thirty square miles of Roundstone Bog, most of them lying in rock-basins, the work of the glaciers that come out of the mountains to the north and pushed across the region, dragging away most of the soil and loose stone, in the last Ice Age. This is what the geologists call knock-and-lochan topography, from the Irish words cnoc, hill, and lochán, lakelet. Hillocks of bare rock stand out among acres of sodden sedgy ground; even the more walkable stretches are a mosaic of heathery hummocks and wet holes.

If Robinson was writing to make the Roundstone Bog seem enticing in a perverse kind of way, I completely understand it. Though I've have not set foot on the Roundstone Bog, over the years I have many times explored the boglands of the Outer Hebrides – a place Robinson recognises as sharing many of the characteristics of the Connemaran terrain. The bogs and hills of South Uist in particular form a landscape in which I've spent many happy hours, running over hills, skirting intricate lochans, not moving all that fast and getting my feet continually soaked through in that wet ground.

While I was reading *Connemara* I spotted the artist Jenny McLaren's painting of the three peaks of South Uist on Instagram.[4] I love the way she works, portraying the landscape and the birdlife found within it onto old maps of the places she paints. When I saw that she had painted the hills onto Ceirinish Bay and Loch Schioport – places on South Uist I know and love – well, that was it really. Those three peaks now hang close to where I write these words; I can look to it, remember and dream.

Along with Robinson's words and McLaren's paintings, I have been thinking of my Auntie Louise, for health reasons now spending her last, pandemic-extended, year in her beloved croft on South Uist. A GP who worked on the Uists for most of her career, she has lived on the eastern side of South Uist for over forty years. First in a small croft on Loch Charnan, fifteen years ago she moved to a larger croft on Loch Eynort in the shadow of Beinn Mor, the highest hill of the island.

Louise loves the Uists for their sense of remoteness and beauty. She first showed me some of these when I was eighteen, at the end of a long summer between A-levels and my first year at university, twenty-five years ago. At the time I'd been running regularly for less than a year, only just beginning to explore moorlands and mountains for myself through climbing, walking and running. She was a good guide; during my first visit she showed me many parts of the islands, their expansive beaches, the machair and the rough bogland that forms much of the terrain, and a few of their small, but perfectly formed hills. I became smitten with it all, and have since kept returning, revisiting places I have come to know well, increasingly exploring more of the archipelago that forms the Western Isles.

I have always come back to the Uists to visit Louise and because of the spell they cast on me. When she soon, very reluctantly, leaves the islands, I will keep returning with my family. As my children grow older we will explore in ways new to them. When we visited last summer my elder daughter paddled a kayak by herself for the first time in the sheltered waters of the loch outside Louise's croft. A warm sunny day, sunlight glistening on the sea, she was thrilled that a few of the seals of the loch came to see us, bobbing alongside our boats, their noses out of the water as they checked us out... 'What are the humans doing now?'

When I was twenty-one, just after my final exams, Aidan and I arrived at Loch Boisdale on the ferry from Oban, our bikes laden with camping and climbing kit. Spending three weeks touring the islands, exploring the beaches, hills and sea cliffs, we camped outside Louise's croft for a week or so. Each morning we would unzip the tent door to look out over Loch Charnain and to the hills rising up from the bog to the south. A chain of three hills each around 600 metres high. While not tall compared to the mountains of the Highlands, they are grand in their place and beautifully formed – Hecla, Beinn Corradail and Beinn Mor, the three peaks of South Uist.

We had each done a couple of fell races and were nominally training to run our first mountain marathon together the following October. On hearing this, Louise told us that traversing the three peaks would be perfect training, that she'd be happy to drop us at one end of the hills and meet us later in the day at the other.

I remember a trip of around twelve miles that felt like twenty, the going was so hard underfoot. I got a big blister on my heel somewhere around Beinn Corradail and was very uncomfortable moving for the rest of the time. If there had been an easy escape route I would have taken it – as it was, the easiest route was the full traverse of the three hills. I didn't appreciate that very much at the time.

Thinking back, this was my first experience of running over the rough terrain underfoot you get on the remoter ground of the Scottish Highlands and Islands. Few paths, the occasional thin line of a deer trod, more often than not bog-trotting and high-stepping over tussock and heather. While it was a rude awakening and may seem strange given my first experience, over the years this kind of running has come to be my most favourite. I don't really think this is due to its difficulty, more the fact that when I am running across such terrain I can pretty much guarantee I am somewhere I love to be.

Each time I have since come to the Uists I have further explored the chain of hills that form the eastern spine of South Uist. One claggy day Louise dropped Aidan and I at Loch Boisdale from where we ran north, following the chain to finish at her croft in Loch Eynort. An atmospheric journey, one of those with poor visibility on and around the tops, making navigation on that intricate ground of bog, little crags, false summits and lochans all the more challenging.

After the trig point marking the summit of the remote hill Stulabhal appeared from the gloom, we descended north-west down a spur towards Loch Shurabhat. The ground was rough and craggy; as we lost height we continually veered here and there, following lines of least resistance until lower, when the rocks diminished and we dropped out of the clag. Despite its dampness the day was warm. With the brown ochre of the bogland under our feet and the grey of the clag above us, I could not see much else. It felt a long way from anywhere; we had not seen a trod or any other kind of path for a couple of miles or so.

We ran gently along the flatter ground. Suddenly, nearby to my left, a large brown thing moved. It took me a few moments to register what it was. A golden eagle. As it flew off its colour, size and finger-tipped wings made this obvious. This place was clearly its domain; it can't have been expecting humans to drop out of the clouds as we did.

After watching the bird leave we carried on, climbing up and over two more hills – Airneabhal and Tinneabhal – before descending a particularly rough stretch of heathery ground as we approached Loch Eynort.

A few days later, this time in clear sunny weather with a light breeze, we climbed Eaval, a pearl of a hill that rises in isolation from the bog on the south-east of North Uist. At just under 350 metres, this hill for me exemplifies why those who gauge the merit of mountains by their height can be so wrong. A rounded peak, it sits imposing on the skyline, anything but diminutive, and the view from the top is something else. The otherwise flatlands of southern North Uist are made up of a multitude of lochans set among the bog. From the summit of Eaval you can gaze out over them and, if your thoughts are not lost in the contrast of sparkling blue lochans and the brown land revealing its deeper colours in the sunlight, you will wonder whether the scene before you is more land or water.

All this treasure and I have still hardly mentioned beachcombing on the wild white beaches on the western coast, the beauty and nature of the machair (the rare grassland set in from the sea on the western side of the islands), the wonder found in gazing out to the Atlantic. I once sat in the sunshine with a pint in my hand outside the pub on the southern tip of South Uist watching a pod of dolphins leap and play together in the Sound of Barra. Another time we were wowed by a huge sea eagle as it flew from the machair towards the mountains. Short-eared owls hunt during the day on the flat boglands of North Uist. I've seen them hovering over the ground, intently looking for prey, deep, all-knowing eyes set into their intense round faces. I could keep writing for a long time about otters, sandpipers, corncrakes, orca whales and more, each doing their own thing in their own wild place. But when I think of the Uists the first thing I see in my mind's eye is the landscape and I recall time spent on lonely Shenaval, the three peaks and Eaval.

I last climbed the three peaks on my thirty-eighth birthday. Aidan and our three-year-old daughter Alanna dropped me at Loch Sgioport and I left them at the road-end, running immediately on to the bog and heading towards Hecla – the first peak.

To begin with I was moving across relatively flat ground, heading more or less due south, passing between a network of lochans before the ground began to rise. Steadily at first, the steepness increased with the height until I left the bog behind, the ground turning to rocky outcrops interspaced with turf, faster going underfoot, but maybe not quite so characterful.

Getting closer to Hecla, its shape steepened as I climbed. The summit is capped by a flat rock tor, giving the impression of a volcano. As I approached the summit cairn I pulled out my compass and played around with it a little. I'd read there is a magnetic anomaly that means you can't trust a bearing at the top of Hecla and I wanted to try it out. The compass did seem to do weird things or it might just have been my imagination. Either way it didn't much matter; it was a clear day and I could see where I was heading next – south-west to a bealach, from where I would climb up to Beinn Corradail.

The descent was good running, mostly short grass where I could get up some speed. Soon enough I found myself in the saddle between the hills, crossing flat ground for a short while before it rose again, my pace slowing with the gradient. As I climbed I looked east, over a blue Loch Coradail to the wilder side of the island. No people or habitation to speak of, bar a lonely lighthouse that I had previously walked out to with Louise.

Like Hecla, the topmost parts of Beinn Corradail are steep and craggy, sheer in places, the easier approach to its summit is on its south or eastern sides. When I reached the cairn I sat down for a while and ate a few jelly babies. Enjoying my time back among the hills of South Uist; this was a true birthday treat. Still to come was another fast and steep descent followed by a final climb up to the summit ridge of Beinn Mor. I was looking forward to the ridge. Unlike the other two peaks Beinn Mor is fin-like, a ridge running north-west to south-east for a mile or so. I traversed it all in perfect sunlight, but for a light mist mainly below me that clung to some of the higher parts of the hill. The Cuillin of Rhum form a claw-like shape on the horizon and, as I looked to them, I remembered time spent on those other mountains. Late afternoon, the air still, sun warm. As I stood at the summit surrounded by the beauty of the Hebrides a perfect feeling of gratitude filled me, for the day and the place I was in. Though fleeting, the moment was mine. Then I was descending rough ground off the southern side of Beinn Mor to Loch Eynort, looking forward to meeting my family for a party tea.

The three peaks of South Uist are a perfect miniature of Scotland's mountains. When among them I find their scale tricks me into thinking they are much larger. They have a stature that belies their height and I seem to move much quicker than normal across them. Or is it me that is the giant? Either way, once you gain height and leave the bog, the grass is short, the going fast.

But in this place, what's the hurry.

3. An Uamh Bhin
The melodious cave

The Isle of Staffa lies four miles off the coast of south-west Mull. A small island of the Inner Hebrides, it gets its name from Old Norse – visiting Vikings were impressed with the basalt columns the island has become famous for and accordingly named it 'Pillar Island'.

The basalt columns run straight, perpendicular to the sea beneath, tightly packed together at an angle that makes the island look like some huge surfacing humpback whale. Intermittently around the cliffs of Staffa, fissures form gaps and caves – the most famous is Fingal's Cave.

The Gaelic name for the cave is *An Uamh Bhin*, meaning 'the melodious cave'. The name Fingal derives in a way from folklore, although it was given to the cave by naturalist Joseph Banks in the eighteenth century. It was said the Irish giant Fionn mac Cumhaill built a bridge between the Giant's Causeway on the north-east coast of Ireland and the cave on Staffa to enable him to travel to Scotland to attack a local giant called Benandonner. Influenced by the legend, Banks named it Fingal's Cave after he 'rediscovered' it in 1772.

The cave has been a source of inspiration to many. Clearly to the Celts who originally named it, through the Scottish Enlightenment to the present day. It's there to be found and explored on the seas of the west coast, surrounded by evocative atmosphere, land and seascapes.

Like so many others, Aidan and I were drawn to Fingal's Cave and wanted to kayak to it. I dreamed about paddling into it to look at the basalt columns on the inside of the cave while floating the water. In practical terms it helps that it's only about five miles from the closest point of the Isle of Mull and the waters surrounding it are calm, at least in calm weather. And we needed calm weather. While we're both reasonably proficient at kayaking, we were inexperienced in rough seas.

I first kayaked in the seas around South Pembrokeshire as a teenager. After a gap of around a decade, I came back to it in my late twenties through racing. At thirty I'd found myself in the front cockpit of a double sea kayak, racing from the island of Rhum to Eigg and then to Arisaig and Loch Morar on the mainland, part of a week-long race in and around the mountains of Lochaber. Thankfully I shared the voyage with a very experienced kayaker and only had to worry about the effort of paddling – he did the rest. I remember a journey of sea breezes, spray in my face as we crested breakers, the feeling of movement in this different place. I enjoyed these feelings and the adventure more than the racing itself, and was bitten by the bug to do more. That summer Aidan and I got our own single sea kayaks. Whenever we visited the coast they came with us, strapped to the roof of our car.

At home in Yorkshire we joined Nidderdale Adventure Club. It was full of seasoned kayakers and canoeists of all kinds. They helped us learn how to roll our boats in the sedate setting of the swimming pool at Harrogate Ladies College. We then went to practise some more off the Northumberland coast near Lindisfarne, paddling with seals on the seaward side of Coquet Island.

On a fine morning the following May we kayaked to Jura to run the hill race over the Paps the following day. Later that summer, at the end of August with a calm weather forecast, we travelled to Mull intending to kayak to Staffa. Arriving near Oban late on a Friday evening, we pitched our tent and slept for a few hours before catching the early morning ferry. It started as a still, clear day with the beginnings of autumn chill, the first one I noticed that year. The sun rose higher as we travelled across the short stretch of water to Craignure on the eastern side of Mull, the horizon and lines around the mountains turning from a rose pink to blue.

From Craignure we headed west on the road to Tobermoray, turning south at Salen towards the mountains and coastline off which Staffa lies. In the decade and more since this initial visit I've come to know this place better. I've watched the sea eagles roost, seen otters swimming and golden-eagles soaring, all the shadow of Ben More, but then it was all new to me. The single-track road curved, rose and dropped with the coastline as we made our way to the jetty by Ulva. Another single-track road does the same on the other side of the loch, the mountains tumble down to meet it.

Ulva is a small island that at its closest point is about fifty metres from Mull. In time we would come back here with our children, catch the little Ulva ferry, visit the seafood café, walk around, explore the island, its history and that of the crofters who used to live there. I found the church a poignant place. Built in 1828 to serve the 570 inhabitants of Ulva, it quickly became less needed when three-quarters of the island's population was cleared in the 1840s. It's still used as a community hall and place of the worship by the fewer than twenty people who live on Ulva today. In the early stages of degeneration, empty now, but with chairs still lined up in rows as pews, you could imagine, almost feel the congregation of people filling the place back in the day.

We parked close to the jetty, took the kayaks off the car roof and carried them down close to the water to load up with kit for the day. By then the sun was high in the sky, the sea sparkling. With a light breeze that would not worry us, off we went, first south along the Sound of Ulva which opens into Loch Na Keal, and then west, following the southern coastline of Ulva.

I was beginning to feel familiar with sea kayaking. The constant bobbing about on the water, how to brace my legs against the walls of the kayak creating the tension that enabled me to use more of my body than just my arms to paddle, my feet controlling the little rudder on the rear of my boat to help me steer.

We made our way across the glistening water, first heading to Little Colonsay, a small island about a mile off the coast of Ulva. It really was flat calm, the kind of conditions where you lose any worries about struggling, having an epic of some kind, meaning we could simply focus on the movement and the places we were going past, towards and through.

Staffa was clear to see, around three miles further to the south-west. The island looked a way off, but getting closer all the while, its profile something I felt familiar with from seeing pictures of it over the years. We could already see the dark shadow in the cliff that marked the entrance to the cave. This is the thing we were aiming for, felt pulled towards, the melodious cave of so many stories.

Occasionally a seal bobbed up to take a look, its curious face wondering about us. Or we'd would see a lone puffin sitting on the water, at home among the ripples and wake of our kayaks. This was their place; they didn't seem to mind us visiting.

At one point I turned to look back up Loch na Keal towards Mull and its mountains, Ben More the highest. They were cast in shadow from the strong sunlight. Had I not been on the water paddling to Staffa, the mountains looked so inviting I would have headed straight to them. Their outline was dark against the blue of the cloudless sky. I wondered what the following day would bring.

As we approached Staffa, I had my biggest wish confirmed. The sea was gently lapping at its cliff walls – those stunning lines of basalt – conditions were calm enough that we would be able to paddle into the cave.

And there it was before us, looking every bit moody and tempting I thought it would. In we went. The sea was so flat, only gently rippling, the cave quiet, the drip of water from my paddle echoed around me. Light shone on the vertical, hexagonal lines of the basalt close to the mouth of the cave; they became shorter and darker the further you go in. Shining our head torches into the darkness towards the cave's end, we explored and looked as much as we could.

How did it feel to be inside the cave? At that moment I'm not sure I would have replied 'melodious' had I been asked. Having previously read of some of the folklore, mythology and romanticism associated with Fingal's Cave, I think I felt the passage of all these stories why this place so inspires. Far enough away to require a journey, close enough so you could see it looking to Staffa from Mull. Mysterious, but within reach.

We had the place to ourselves for a while, but of course the cave wasn't ours alone and a ferry load of people arrived, almost breaking the spell. Deciding to take a look at more of Staffa, we left the cave, paddling a short distance northwards and then towards the jetty where the ferry was by then mooring against. Landing our kayaks on a rocky beach, I pulled off my spray-deck and got out to take a walk. After sitting in the kayak, bracing and steering for so long, my legs felt funny to start with and it took a little while for them to return to normality as I moved.

The highest point on Staffa is at forty-two metres, a trig point close by. From there we took in the view – first back to Mull, its mountains and coastline, Ulva in the foreground, then westwards, towards the Treshnish Isles, a line of small islands around five miles north-west of Staffa. There was no real hurry, so we sat for a time to take it all in.

Getting back into the boats, we decided on a circumnavigation of Staffa before taking one last look into Fingal's Cave. Continuing anticlockwise, seeing yet more of its basalt lines, other caves in the cliffs, just marvelling at it all really. When we reached the opening to the cave for the second time, we just had to go back in. Again there were other people looking, having followed a little path along the lower basalt stacks at the bottom of the cliff from the jetty.

By mid-afternoon we had to leave. Returning to Ulva we took a slightly different line, this time passing to the north of Little Colonsay and then following the coastline of Ulva more closely. This brought us close to the multitude of little islands that lie in the middle of Ulva's southern coastline. At one of them we decided to stop for a brew, pulling the kayaks up onto a rock edge, getting the stove out of a hatch, we soon had a hot cup of tea. About fifty metres away a seal lay snoozing in the sun, after waking and taking a look at us it realised we were no threat and went back to sleep.

After tea and biscuits, we only had to follow the coastline east for a few miles to reach the Sound of Ulva. Even though the weather had been benign the whole day it still felt reassuring that we'd not far to go. We could completely relax; even if freak weather blew in we'd be fine.

Soon enough we were back at the quay on Mull. The Ulva ferry had stopped for the day; we paddled alongside, pulled our kayaks out of the water and began to unpack all the kit. There were a couple of children crabbing from the quay; I must have made a mental note about this as we have come back with our two to do the same.

That morning we'd passed a small campsite at the head of Loch na Keal. We went there, pitched our tent and were soon cooking dinner in the long light of the evening, looking across the water to Ben More which we planned to climb the following day. As the sun went down we ate, drank a beer, and then slept.

We woke to a change in the weather. Drizzle pattered onto the tent, the mountains were wreathed in grey. As we climbed Ben More up and down the popular route there wasn't much of a view – we could have been anywhere. Never mind, we had been quite somewhere the day before and on the Islands you have to take the rough with the smooth.

This kayak to Staffa was the first time Aidan and I had visited Mull. We've been back a few times since then with our children. Our last visit was for a week in August two years ago. Late one afternoon during that trip I rode my bike on a loop from Salen around the coastal and mountain roads of central and western Mull. Passing underneath Ben More, continuing along the road west and then following it to climb hairpins to the road pass between the Ben More massif and the crags on the side of Fionna Mham. At the high-point on the road I stopped and looked out to the west. The sun was twinkling on the sea, I had a perfect view to Staffa and could just make out the shadow of the cave. Our kayak trip had been a decade before to the day. In some ways it felt a lifetime ago. I have a yearning to kayak back to Staffa, sometime I will. As I rode my bike in the afternoon sunshine around the mountains, it was enough to know it was there.

4. An Teallach
A world away

A late May afternoon in central Leeds, a Friday. I'd been working too many hours, become too obsessed with a project I was working on. Aidan had phoned some of the people I worked with at the time to get them to help make sure I left the office at 2pm. He picked me up and we started the long drive north, away to the mountains.

Sunny and warm, the forecast was set fair for the weekend. As we drove away from Yorkshire, past the Lake District and into Scotland, I felt the layers of pressure I had been putting myself under begin to peel away. Beyond the central belt, heading up the A9 and away from home, work felt more distant, began to feel less important.

We were heading to the north-west, but had decided to break up the journey with a bivvy on the hill. Parking the car in a lay-by close to the Dromochter Pass, we climbed the hillside towards the rounded summit of Càrn na Caim, one of the two Munros close to each other on the eastern side of the road.

The evening was very still. The view from the summit was hazy. Somewhere above our heads a skylark sang. A welcome sound, but I remember thinking it was late – surely the bird should be sleeping. Maybe they don't sleep much that time of year; while it was past nine o' clock we still had daylight and it would be light a fair while yet. I looked out over the mountains all around, silhouetted against the late evening sky, layer upon layer, each lighter in colour as their distance from us grew.

My own tiredness began to catch up with me. Our plan was to find a bivvy spot somewhere between the summit we were standing on and that of A' Bhuidheanach Bheag, a summit a few miles south that we would head to when we woke the following morning.

The terrain of the ground between the two summits was tussocky and rough. From Càrn a Caim we followed a trod until the ground started to look more comfortable to sleep on. Pulling out sleeping and bivvy bags along with a roll mat to sleep on from our rucksacks, we also got out our little stove, brewed up some hot chocolate and watched the sunset behind Ben Alder, dozing off into the half-light.

Through the night I felt myself get colder. The wind started up; soon it began to feel like it was drizzling, although really it was just cloud forming around us. While my bivvy bag wasn't leaking I became increasingly uncomfortable. At around 5am we gave up trying to sleep, packed our kit together and started to head towards A' Bhuidheanach Bheag.

Visibility was minimal. We were moving on the compass, having taken a bearing. As we approached the summit, within about half a mile of it, Aidan suggested we leave our packs by the side of the track as we'd be coming back the same way. He always looks for ways to save a bit of energy, but I don't know why I thought that was a good idea. Half an hour later we were still looking for the summit, moving around in circles off the track. Tired, hungry and bagless. Stopping still for a little while, I took a further look at our map. Using my compass I lined it up to north and attempted to work out our location given the direction, shape and steepness of the land around us, trying to fit them to the contours of the map.

Giving up on the summit, we focused on finding our bags. Having estimated roughly where we were, I suggested to Aidan we headed due north until we hit the track we had lost and then followed it as it gently curved north-west, to the cairn we had left them beside. Success. Swinging them onto our backs, we continued downhill back towards the car, despite our dithering with luck we'd make it to Kinlochewe in time for the start of the Slioch Hill Race.

At the time I didn't really know very much about Slioch or the wonders of the mountains around it. *Slioch* is Gaelic for spear. Looking to it from the south-west, the shore of Loch Maree, this mountain dominates the skyline – imperious – facing south out of the Great Wilderness, towering over the water. Starting in Kinlochewe, the twelve-mile route of the hill race runs along the River Kinlochewe to the head of Loch Maree, after which it follows the natural horseshoe formed by Slioch and its ridges.

I'd spent time in Glen Carron and Torridon, but not travelled to the mountains further north into the Great Wilderness and beyond. In the years since then I have done so. Not nearly as much as I would like, but now I know more. As I write these words, reminding myself of the landscape by looking at maps, remembering journeys, sketching some of the scenes I have seen, I feel a yearning for the place. It's been a long time.

The weather improved that day as soon as we dropped a few hundred metres below the tops of the Drumochter Hills. To the north were clear skies and sunshine. We pressed on down to the car to keep on with our journey up the A9 to Inverness from where we'd turn west, on the road to Acnasheen and then to Kinlochewe.

Arriving at the edge of the village, we followed signs to the race start and I registered to run. Aidan planned to climb Slioch to see me somewhere on my way around. Already warm in the glen and with no wind, for the duration of the race it was only going to get hotter. I got into race kit, rubbing sun cream into my arms, shoulders and legs. The race soon began and with around a hundred other runners I began to make my way around the route.

It's fair to say that a fitful night's sleep on a mountainside wasn't the best preparation. I'm also rubbish at racing in hot weather. I knew all that but didn't really care, I just wanted to cram as many mountains and time spent on them into the weekend. Tired and dehydrated before I started, in the heat of the race I struggled with cramp. I made my way painfully around theroute, reaching the top of Slioch, running through it along the horseshoe.

I didn't really take in the mountains around me and even ran past Aidan without seeing him.

I don't have any particular memories, only of the heat and the wild goats soon after I left the edge of Loch Maree. There was a small herd standing among boulders about fifty metres from the trod before I began the climb of Slioch proper. I smelt them too – that unmistakable aroma which always brings back memories of climbing up through the Llanberis slate quarries in North Wales on the way up Elidir Fawr. This time, on my way up a different mountain, hundreds of miles from Snowdonia, the smell was the same.

The goats looked at me with inquisitive eyes. Probably they'd have asked what the hell I was doing. With salt from my sweat running into and stinging my eyes, along with the beginnings of what would become painful cramp in my hamstrings and calves, I wasn't sure I really had any form of rational answer.

While I've climbed Slioch, it didn't really feel the same to the ways I have climbed and spent time on many other hills in the north-west. During the years since the race I have read about Slioch, sketched it, painted it, looked to it from the edge of Loch Maree as I visited on trips to go other places. Although now I feel like I know it better, as I'm writing I'm feeling a strong urge to visit this mountain again. There is a lot to be said for racing around mountains, but one of the negatives about passing over them at speed is that you just don't get the time to properly look.

At the finish I needed to sit in the race field and drink electrolyte to steadily rehydrate. Aidan found me feeling sorry for myself and chastised me – it had been my choice to race after all. He was right, but and it had been a great route and race – I was just in a bad state for running it.

By then it was late afternoon, the air beginning to cool a little. We needed somewhere to rest and sleep. A runner told us about a campsite at Gairloch in the sand dunes on the edge of a white beach about twenty miles west of Kinlochewe, along Loch Maree and to the north-west. We decided to head there and stop at the Kinlochewe stores to buy some food for dinner along the way.

As Aidan drove I looked at the scenery and also the map I had unfolded in front of me. We were skirting the southern edge of the Fisherfield Wilderness, an expansive area of mountains also known as the Great Wilderness. This was somewhere I had heard about, but not spent much time researching – reading about mountains and ridges new to me, looking at maps of the area back home. As I sat in the car I translated the map unfolded in my lap to the mountains we were passing on the other side of Loch Maree. I began to realise that this was quite some place. Though I'd run up Slioch I'd only been to the edge of it and I wanted to explore and feel it some more.

41

We found the campsite near Gairloch and pitched the tent facing west, looking out over the beach and across The Minch beyond to the Outer Hebrides. The sun hadn't set, but I didn't think I'd last long enough to see it drop down below the horizon. After a dinner of pasta and half a bottle of beer, I felt an overwhelming tiredness and fell fast asleep listening to the sound of the breakers.

I woke with sunrise. Getting out of the tent I looked out across the sea to the horizon and then back across the sleeping campsite. Aidan was awake too and we quietly took down the tent. It was going to be another fine day and we did not want to waste any time. One of the final things we had spoken of before we had fallen asleep the night before was where to head the following morning. Spoiled for choice between one of the great Torridon ridges or An Teallach on the northern edge of the Fisherfield Wilderness. What a decision to have to make as we'd not climbed any of them. Aidan was torn between Laitach or An Teallach, but it didn't take much persuasion to choose the latter; he felt the same as me. Smitten the evening before, looking at the map as we drove along Loch Maree, I wanted to see more of the mountains of the Great Wilderness.

Leaving the campsite on the road north-east, we headed for the village of Dundonnell at the foot of An Teallach. This ribbon of a road follows the coastline, first heading north and then east along Little Loch Broom in swoops and bends, climbing to high points, then dropping down to sea level. That morning was my first time along it. A few years later I would cycle it, ride the forty miles from Gairloch to meet the Ullapool–Inverness road at the Braemore junction and then on, towards Achnasheen to Glen Carron. Starting with the swoopiness of the coast after Gairloch, from Dundonnell it climbs up through Dundonnell Gorge and over the Fain Bridge to reach a high point close to the Fain Bothy, where the views to the mountains – An Teallach in particular – are expansive.

Soon after I cycled it I discovered this road has a name – The Destitution Road. What a name for such a place of beauty; so named because it was built during the devastating potato famines of the 1840s. Local workers built it in exchange for food. In the Highlands there are a number of such roads – the men, women and children who built them would receive rations of oats in return for their hard graft. Imagine how it must have been to build roads by hand in the often harsh Highland conditions, living at the point of starvation. When I cycled it, loving the scenery and the challenge of the ride, I didn't know to give this a second thought.

Despite our early start that early May morning, there were a few other cars parked in the lay-bys close to Dundonnell House. We figured these belonged to people who had gone further into the Fisherfields for the weekend, maybe staying at the Shenavall bothy. From where we parked we could see the ridgelines of An Teallach and the peaks of this range, the jagged Sgùrr Fiona, pointed Bidean a' Ghlas Thuill and the more rounded Stob Cadha Gobhlaich. Some judge this range to be the Highland's finest and that morning I could understand why.

We parked near the end of a rough stony track that heads south-west and followed this for a few miles, gently climbing, passing through natural woodland and over more open ground. It was a still morning, so much so there was no real sound apart from the noise we both made as we jogged along.

The track we were running along makes its way over the eastern shoulder of An Teallach, climbing to a height of around 400 metres before dropping into Strath na Sealga. Aidan and I would not descend into this glen, but at the apex of the track we turned north-west instead to properly begin the climb of Sail Liath and the southern end of An Teallach. As we did so I looked around to see mountains everywhere. The Fannichs, Fisherfields, Slioch and more. Immediately in front of us, on the far side of Strath na Sealga, was Beinn Dearg Mòr, quite possibly one of the most beautifully shaped mountains I had ever seen. A triple-peaked ridge with one main coire, cast into deep shadow by the sun shining from the east.

We were on the edge, looking over and into these places. I had yet to climb these hills, to explore them, get to know them. These are such concentrated mountains you could move across them all at a pace over maybe two days, faster if you really wanted to, but I wanted to eke them out, to experience them fully with all my senses, and to make these experiences last.

I knew the Shenaval bothy was not far from where we stood, low down in the strath, facing out towards Beinn Dearg Mòr. The following Easter Aidan and I camped close to the bothy for a few nights, climbing the Fisherfields, Beinn Dearg Mòr and just generally hanging out. Another time we explored the Fannichs, wild camping over a couple of days.

All that was yet to come. I had no idea how and when I would travel into these mountains, but felt sure I would. I was surprised at the calmness I felt when thinking this. Instead of my then typical style of wanting to try to bag them all in one long day, I felt a need to do them more slowly, to eke out the time I would spend travelling amongst them and climbing them. I looked to them that morning with a kind of anticipatory thrill.

And before all of those hills there was An Teallach. We left the track, climbing steeply, steadily getting higher, approaching Sail Liath and the ridge of the range. While I think I remember a trod on the ground, at least in places, this was one of those tough steep climbs you just have to get on with as the ridge arrives soon enough.

As I paced upwards, in my own little world of hard work and heavy breathing, I remember thinking just how far I felt removed from the challenges of my job, all the thinking I needed to do. and the frustrations I was feeling. When I was at work it all felt so important, but climbing that mountainside, my feelings of complete irrelevance when surrounded by such peaks helped me to see it all in context. As if on cue I heard a cuckoo calling from somewhere lower down, telling me to live in the moment.

The climb begins to taper off and the ridge tightens approaching 800 metres. Soon we reached Sail Liath, the first summit and then carried on along the ridge. I remember a warm day but a cool breeze and we weren't moving as fast as I did over Slioch, so I didn't get hot and uncomfortable. The ground was dry, dusty rather than muddy. The rock is red and sticky – Torridonian sandstone – good friction with the fell shoes I was wearing. Along the scrambly parts of the ridge this helped my confidence as I felt the exposure, the way the ground steeply dropped away from ether side of the rocky crest we were following towards the summit of Sgùrr Fiona.

After Sgùrr Fiona came Bidean a Ghlas Thuill, the highest peak of the range. After this, while the main ridgeline continued north-east, there was also a ridgeline running due east to the outlying peak Glas Mheall Liath. Aidan wanted to bag it but I wasn't all that bothered, preferring to sit down and wait the half hour or so it took him. As I watched him traverse the ground he steadily became silhouetted against the horizon. Hazy light, beyond him was layer upon layer of mountains. This dreamy scene and the warmth from the sun felt soporific, as I sat there relaxing I ended up dozing for a while.

When he returned we continued to the end of the range at Glas Mheall Mor, retracing our steps a little to drop down into Coire a' Ghlas Thule, then following the burn back down towards Dundonnell. The descent was fast and not overly steep, so I could stretch out my stride and run free. The breeze added a gentle coolness to the air, close to perfect spring conditions in the Highlands.

A mile or so before the road, our path passed a waterfall. About twenty feet high and free flowing into its own plunge pool, it looked an incredibly inviting place for a swim. I quickly undressed and jumped in. Aidan was more cautious; he doesn't handle cold water all that well. As he stood on the edge, tiptoeing the water, he pointed at a dipper in profile at the top of the falls – a beautiful brown bird with a cream bib. It flitted around the water, keeping away from us but watching from a safe distance. I wondered if its nest was behind the falls.

The water soothed my tired legs and sunburned arms. I dived under, felt the intense cold, my whole body shocked at first and then I relaxed into how refreshed this made me feel. I think I was finally beginning to properly unwind. Into the mountains it was a world away from the bullshit and hubbub, the normalised behaviours and processes we'd left behind – for the weekend at least.

We could have stayed by that pool for much longer, but left all too soon to follow the path down to the road where we'd begun our day, through a forested area overgrown with rhododendrons. Popping out on the tarmac, we had a mile or so to walk back to the lay-by we had parked our car. Physically tired, but mentally refreshed after these days and nights of mountains, we took it in turns to drive the long way back south.

5. Flowerdale
Looking

Not normal.
But you are overlooked,
Smothered by taller ridges
You sit there, quietly in the tundra
An afterthought?
Not for me

I see you.
Through the thin grey light, across dull brown land
I see you
A spell is cast
I dream of you

Your shapes rising up from the flat bog
Curves and lines that meet in round summits
I feel your shape, your stature
The reassurance in your presence

You announce your arrival on the skyline quietly
Only heard by those who want to listen
The problem is you're just not tall enough
Maybe that's your trick

Aidan and I leave the car park and I start running. I'm always keen to start at a decent pace – Aidan not so bothered. After an hour or so of the gap between us yo-yoing, he'll speed up and I'll slow down. We'll meet somewhere in the middle, but before that happens I think each of us is content to goad the other into changing speed – we've been doing it for years.

I feel excited; we're back in the mountains and today we'll be traversing a ridge we've both wanted to climb for ages. Beinn Eighe. This is a famous line along with Liathach and Beinn Alligin, and it's one of Torridon's three classic mountain traverses. We climbed Beinn Alligin two days ago, on a clear day with a dusting of snow above around 800 metres. It's November and the weather has been mixed. Yesterday it was rubbish and now, though there's clag on the tops, it's due to clear and we hope to get a view from the ridge.

Our approach is from the west and we'll run through and up out of Coire Mhic Fhearchair (past the famous Triple Buttress), gaining the ridge at the bealach between Ruadh-stac Mór and Coinneach Mhór. From the car park this gives us a few miles of relatively easy climbing to the saddle of a wide bealach – Coire Dubh Mor – to continue around the western end of Beinn Eighe and then into Coire Mhic Fhearchair.

My legs are feeling good and I keep up a fair pace. As we climb the path, on my right I have the steep ramparts of Beinn Eighe, to my left the eastern end of Liathach. The clag is down to about 600 metres so I can't see much of them. But I can feel them around me, like we're moving into the mountains.

The gradient eases as we approach Coire Dubh Mor. It's a classic low bealach, wide and flat, boggy underfoot with small lochans. Around us are boulders, small and large, the path weaves between and around them. Torridonian sandstone, brown rock with a pink hue, adds a gentle colour to this day of dull light.

At the cairn that marks the saddle-point I pause to take a breather and wait for Aidan; he's not too far away. He passes me and speeds on ahead, leaving me behind and winding me up. I follow.

After the saddle, the path takes a slight rising contour, steadily beginning to turn eastwards along the lower section of Sàil Mhor, one of the peaks of Beinn Eighe. We've passed the end of Laithach and now have the massif of Beinn Dearg on our left. Eventually we clear this and get a view out to the north-west to some hills.

Some hills. Behind them a line of grey ocean, in front a few miles of flat brown tundra and a group of lochans. Wisps of cloud linger around their summits. There are three hills, grouped together, but separate from one another, not connected by ridges. From where I stand there is no clear path to them; the ground between us seems wilder, and this feeling is reflected in the perception I have of them. Wild, lonely mountains, rising up from the tundra. There's a calm stature about them, their shape and that feeling stays with me, captured in memories that will last for years.

Aidan and I carried on to climb Beinn Eighe. The mist was still down as we passed the triple buttress in Coire Mhic Fhearchair so it was hidden from us. For a while the mist moved about us, sometimes above, sometimes below, giving a feeling of other-worldliness. Given the grey moraine and pink quartzite of the ridge, we could have entered a portal to some kind of moonscape. But, as we climbed the steep scree slope up out of the coire to join the ridge, the mist cleared steadily.

We traversed Beinn Eighe, experienced the ridge on an atmospheric day and appreciated the beauty of the line and its peaks. What stayed with me more than anything, however, was that view of those three hills. I later discovered that these are the three peaks of the Flowerdale Forest – Beinn a' Chearcaill, Beinn an Eòin and Baosbheinn. Reaching 875 metres at their highest point, they are not Munros and so they see fewer human hill-goers. They feel wilder and more remote for it.

If I had to think of any one thing that triggered the desire in me to paint mountains that moment was it. Those three hills haunt me. At home in Yorkshire I can close my eyes and see them still today. More than that, there was a little voice in my head (that grew louder) willing me to paint them on a big canvas with oils, something I'd never done before or had even thought about.

The following spring I went back to run a two-day mountain marathon from Gairloch with my friend Andrea. I was delighted when I found that we would spend much of our time running around and about Flowerdale. While I was supposed to have my head down racing, much to the bemusement of Andrea, I kept looking to the mountains. The sun shone all weekend, casting strong shadows on the hills and deepening their spell. Afterwards, as we drove back south along the western end of Loch Maree, we stopped so I could capture the view to Beinn an Eòin and Baosbheinn.

That photograph would, just a few weeks later, while standing at an easel in my bedroom in Yorkshire, become my first painting. With this I found my way back to the mountains. It felt magical, like alchemy.

6. Christmas in Lochaber
Crossing the Abhainn Rath

For a few years around a decade ago, Aidan and I spent each
Christmas somewhere in the Highlands. In settled weather the
low, clear light of winter made for memorable days in the hills.
One year we stayed with friends at a bunkhouse in Kinlochleven,
which is a perfect base from which to explore some of the
mountains of the Highland region of Lochaber. Sitting in the
glen below the Mamores, it's also within easy reach of Glencoe
and the mountains of the Nevis Range.

Reaching the Highlands a few days before Christmas Eve and
having a spell of calm weather, we spent all our time in the
mountains. At the time my fitness was such that I could run and
run and do it all again the next day. That was also all I wanted to
do, which was at times frustrating for Aidan. Plenty fit enough
for long consecutive days in the hills, but not necessarily fit
enough to run all of them and he didn't feel the desire to just
pass over the mountains as fast as he could. He did, however,
want to bag as many Munros as possible. We resolved on a
compromise: some days we spent together, some on our own,

and sometimes we would climb the first mountain or two together and then split off to go our own way.

In the two days before Christmas we headed into the Grey Corries and Mamores. On Boxing Day we climbed Sgòr na h-Ulaidh and Stob an Fhuarain, two of the outlying summits of Glencoe. The day after that we had a particularly memorable time on the Creag Meagaidh plateau, above a cloud inversion in dazzling sunlight. On Christmas Day itself, after two days on the hill, Aidan chose a rest day. I'd brought a bike with me, and wanted to explore the trails that head east from Kinlochleven.

After a little planning, I decided on a route. Perhaps the most obvious, though maybe a little long for the time of year and amount of daylight. There's a natural line, a circuit, on tracks and trails that skirts the whole of the Mamores and Nevis ranges. Just under fifty miles and I could start early. The ground was in a fine condition for riding – cold, solid ground, no snow lower down. While I would need to avoid icy patches, these should be fairly sparse as it had been dry for a while.

I left Kinlochleven just before daybreak in the dim light that comes before it. First climbing steeply up a path close to the Grey Mare's Tail waterfall to gain flatter ground and the track that that would take me along the southern edge of the Mamores, past Loch Eilde Mor and Loch Eilde Beag. The track was fast going. I spun along in the low light, breaking the ice on some of the puddles along the way and cautiously skittering over others. Daylight came as I rode along. It crept up slowly, until I realised the morning had properly begun. My body was warmed with the effort of climbing the trail; although the air was cold, I felt cosy inside my layers.

As I write these words, twelve years after this Christmas bike ride, the memories are so strong I can feel that body heat. Some people say you can remember a place you love more vividly when you are at a distance and, for whatever reason, you cannot return. At home in Yorkshire, in the confined world of a Covid winter, I can feel the cold, low-lit air around me and my body becoming warmer with the exertion of riding uphill. In order to help me remember even more, I pull out my map of these mountains, to look at the line of this bike ride. It's not that I have forgotten, but I know looking at my map will help me to feel the shape of the land again.

The route was a full tour of the perimeter of the Mamores, Ben Nevis, Aonachs and Grey Corries. While the Mamores are their own separate massif, the Aonachs and Grey Corries are linked to Ben Nevis by high bealachs, forming one massif dominated by the Ben at its western end. The Mamores and Ben Nevis Range are separated by Glen Nevis, down which runs the Water of Nevis that rises at the eastern end of the Mamores.

Ten summers after this Christmas bike ride I would attempt to run the Tranter's Round, the classic mountain challenge that traverses all these summits in a horseshoe of Glen Nevis. As I look to the map I am reminded of these two and other journeys, the nature of the landscape, the way I felt as I moved across it. But more than anything else the map reminds me of the starkness of these mountains. The tight contours and abstract three-dimensional shapes, ridgelines rising to meet at summits, separated by the space formed by water. As I read the map I feel again their immense bulk and stature around me, reminding me of feeling tiny and unimportant as I rode my bike around these giants, and of how that had felt just fine...

Back on that Christmas Day, the track continued to run fast under my wheels. Soon enough I knew it would become less smooth, slower going. I didn't think I would have enough time to ride the whole of the route in daylight and was glad to be making fast progress while I could.

After the two Loch Elides, the track climbs up a little more before descending to meet the Abhainn Rath. This river rises the other side of the watershed from the Water of Nevis, flowing eastwards for around six miles where it then forms the main inflow of Loch Trieg. The Abhainn Rath is a river that quickly becomes impassable in poor weather as water pours down the mountainsides that surround it. On the route I'd planned it was something I needed to cross. With no bridge over the river, I would have to either wade across it or detour around Meall Mór, an outlying peak of the Grey Corries, easily adding an hour onto my journey. Though I wanted to cross direct if I could, I was a little nervous about this despite the dry weather of the previous few days.

Looking eastwards, down the glen formed by the Abhainn Rath and then beyond, through the next gap in the mountains where the trainline runs past the remote Corrour Station, I could see the edge of Rannoch Moor. For most of the day cloud hung heavy above me, generally higher than the mountaintops but making for a grey day low of light. For a moment, however, looking that way, weak sunlight broke this cloud and shone down on the moor. The land became more colourful.

I'd been that way just the previous month, when spending a weekend with Aidan on the eastern side of moor close to Rannoch Station. In similar conditions we had climbed Sgòr Gaibhre and Càrn Dearg, two hills of the Rannoch Forest. With a thin layer of snow from around 700 metres, these mountains had that classic look – white higher up, ochre brown below. In-between Rannoch and Corrour stations, the trainline passes over the wide open land of Rannoch Moor. As we descended south westwards off Càrn Dearg, taking a line to the Old Corrour Lodge and the track we would follow back to our starting point, a train passed by on its way to Fort William. How little it looked. I imagined the people inside... were they pressing their faces to the windows, wiping off steam from the warmth of the carriage and gazing out, as I would have been? I waved at them a bit hopelessly, even if anyone was looking our way there was little chance of them spotting us. We were two people on a hillside a long way above them, watching this little sign of humanity pass by, a little bemused by its presence in this place.

Another time I caught the train from Bridge of Orchy to Rannoch with my friend Andrea. We normally climb mountains, but I'd suggested we explore the moor a little. It was a claggy day; we didn't get to see all that much. I mostly remember the old tree roots preserved in the peat of the bog. As we ran I spent some time thinking what this place would have been like when the trees were standing. I assume they were Caledonian pines, part of the great old forest, long gone in this deerstalkers' land...

It felt colder as I picked up speed on my bike, descending the trail towards the Abhainn Rath. On the other side of the river, I could see the Meanach bothy. A small building in the middle of nowhere, red painted door and window frames contrasting with the dull greens and browns of the land around. I would pass by on my way to Lairig Leacach, the glen that runs along the eastern edge of the Grey Corries. From this distance the bothy looked both lonely and welcoming. I wondered whether there would be anyone staying there, spending their nights in a place that felt a million miles away from the consumerism that drives Christmas these days.

Sometimes you have to go a long way from something to look at it objectively, to assess it. That morning, descending into and crossing this lonely glen, I felt a long way away from Christmas Day. Choosing to spend much of it alone, in traversing this remote place I had plenty of time to think. I didn't really spend much of it thinking what Christmas means to me, but I did continually appreciate that state of mind that physical exertion combined with wide-open beauty takes me.

But what does Christmas mean to me? My mum tried to instil in me a Christian faith. I have always respected her beliefs, but I used to sit with her in church on Sundays, wondering what it was that led these people to pray to an entity I could not find in myself the ability to believe in, despite often wanting to. I stopped going to church as soon as I was old enough to assert free will on this matter and concluded long ago that if I'm going to worship anything, I will find it in the land.

Which brings me to paganism. It seems to me that, more than anything, this is a religion in touch with the land and the natural world. I know that this is more than just worshipping the sun, but doesn't it make sense to glorify the thing that gives us life? I don't think I believe in anything other than that the Earth is a complex natural system – Gaia – within which humans are currently playing a defining and destructive part. While this is a scientific viewpoint, of all the religions, paganism seems closest to this.

I want to celebrate the old Yule. Take away the buying and consuming and the new religions, and what you find is a celebration of the winter solstice, the turning of the season, and the passing of the year. Old beliefs and ways like celebrating Yule stemmed from a need to live in contact with the land and local environment, something lost through industrialisation. The lives and wellbeing of our ancestors depended on understanding and respecting the natural world, the threats and opportunities that existed alongside them.

In her book *Folklore of the Scottish Highlands*, Anne Ross writes of how the Celts – the earliest inhabitants of the Highlands – knew and loved the area in which they lived so very well.[5] Many of their stories, the folklore that Ross researched in depth and writes of, are derived from this knowledge:

Every place had its name and its legend – how it got its name; what famous hero or infamous criminal, savage, supernatural animal, or shaggy, semi-human sprite associated with it, were stories known at one time to all. This Celtic obsession with immediate locality, the love and knowledge of not only the homeland, but every detail of the familiar landscape, is an absolutely fundamental characteristic of the Celts.

These names and legends were stories and secrets, shared by word of mouth, passing down each generation and slowly becoming forgotten by many as ways of living changed.

One of the secrets we have lost is our connection to the land. Wrapping the old winter festivals in jaunty paper and smothering them with new religions has been one of the routes to this forgetfulness.

I wasn't thinking these or any other deep thoughts when I reached the Abhainn Rath though. The river was kind. When I came to cross it was shallow, unthreatening, and the highest the water came was up to my knees. Having read other people's accounts of waist-deep crossings, I was thankful to get only a little wet. The water was icy cold and I was unsteady with the bike hooked over my shoulder, but in no real danger of a drenching.

Continuing to shoulder the bike, I crossed boggy ground towards the rough path to take me up to the pass. I was thankful the ground was mostly frozen solid, a few degrees warmer and my already sodden feet would be sinking into the muddy bog that formed much of the trod.

Passing close to the Meanach bothy there were no signs of life. If anyone was staying in this bothy maybe they were out on the hill. So, no one else around, probably for miles. Instead of feeling lonely, I felt the peace of the place. This calm day with little to no wind, meant my own movements and breathing were the only things I could hear. After crossing the bog, I began to climb to the pass, my body becoming warmer again through the effort.

A small lochan marks the high point of the shallow bealach I was crossing, lying between Stob Bàn, the furthest south of the larger mountains of the Grey Corries, and Meall Mór. From this vantage point I could see down into Lairig Leacach, and along its length as it descends north-west towards Spean Bridge. Translated from the Gaelic, *Lairig Leacach* means flat valley. Downstream it is tight and narrow, opening out to wider ground higher up the glen. I could imagine the importance of this place to the people who named it – a hanging hidden valley where sanctuary, greater safety and a place of rest could be found in times of need.

At the lochan I unhooked my bike from my shoulder and started to ride again, slow at first and then faster as the ground steepened when I approached the floor of the glen. I let go a little and enjoyed the speed, always keeping my eyes on the trail ahead, negotiating rocks and drops along the way, wary of icy patches which could take my wheels out from under me. Descending into the glen brought me to another bothy – Leacach. Again there was nobody around, but familiar signs of life were there: frozen studmarks from Aidan's fell-running shoes and mine when we'd passed two days before on our way up into the hills.

What time was it then? As I write these memories I try to remember, not all that surprised I have forgotten as I always lose track of time when I'm in the hills. Probably a little after 1pm. Not enough daylight left to complete the ride in the light, but I always knew that was likely to be the case.

At the bothy the path down the glen turns into fast double track. I rolled down the narrowing ground to the edge of the pine forest that lines the lower parts of the northern slopes of the Nevis range. Crossing through the deer fence, the trail became faster again – the smooth gravel of a forest road.

I'd planned to follow the line of the old railway west through the forest to Torlundy, a small village close to Fort William, but instead decided on the faster option of the A82, one of the main trunk roads of the Highlands. Soon enough I was passing by Spean Bridge, clicking along the miles with the Aonachs and Ben Nevis over my left shoulder.

Given the holiday, the road was quiet, but as I approached the edge of Fort William, I passed a petrol station that was open and surprisingly busy. Back at the hut we needed some milk so I stopped to buy some. It felt odd to do that on Christmas Day and even stranger when I contrasted here to where I'd been all day. Bright lights, bustling people, beeping cash till – all so familiar – *had I really just been somewhere else, somewhere different?*

In a few hours I would be making and eating dinner, sharing festivities with Aidan and our friends back in the hut. Before this, though, and knowing I would have to fix my lights to my handlebars somewhere along the trail, was the final stretch of my ride. I continued along the main road to the roundabout at the edge of the centre of Fort William. Turning left up Glen Nevis, I soon reached the end of the West Highland Way to follow this south-east, over a low shoulder of the Mamores to Kinlochleven in the dying midwinter light.

7. The Five Sisters of Kintail

Above the inversion

In the Western Highlands, close to Skye, the Five Sisters of Kintail are five mountains that together form a striking chain. Sentinels of Glen Shiel at its western end, rising up from the head of Loch Duich, they are one of the Highland's most well-known and recognisable lines of hills.

I had admired the Five Sisters for years, seen them from a distance as I climbed and moved about other mountains in Glen Affric, Knoydart, Mullardoch and Skye's Cuillin. Passing them often on the road to Glen Carron, Torridon, Skye and the islands, each time I would look to the Five Sisters and remind myself that one day I would have to stop and take myself along this famous ridge.

I was also fascinated by the name. It seemed romantic and fitting. Five beautiful pointed mountains that rise up and come together to form a ridge, linking hands by bealachs. But what's

in a name; how did these Five Sisters come to be? I researched it a little. According to legend these five mountains are indeed sentinels of sorts.

One of the Kings of Old Kintail had seven daughters, but no sons. The youngest two both married Irish princes and were allowed by their father to leave his kingdom, to sail away to Ireland with their husbands. The two princes told the King they had five brothers whom they promised would sail to Kintail and marry his other daughters. The four of them sailed away and were never seen again. The other five sisters waited in vain. To preserve their beauty until the princes arrived, a Grey Magician promised the King he would turn them to stone. These are the sisters who stand, gazing to the west, still waiting for their princes to come.

If I am honest, this irritated me. In my initial ignorance of their backstory I'd imagined the Five Sisters to be Amazonian in their stature and strength, standing proud at the edge of Kintail to always protect their people and to ward off threats. Maybe I shouldn't have delved, kept my own idea of the story intact.

One July, when our first daughter was a year old, Aidan and I stayed with her and his parents on the side of Loch Long, close to Dornie and Loch Duich, a few miles from the Five Sisters. Early on a grey, overcast morning Aidan teased me that I'd still not climbed these mountains. He had done them a couple of years before, while I spent a weekend racing around the mountains of Kintail and Glen Affric rather than summit bagging like him. He suggested he drop me at one end of the ridge and pick me up at the other a few hours later. Not one to pass up such an opportunity, I quickly packed a bit of kit and got in the car.

Despite my not having climbed the Five Sisters at that time, Kintail and its neighbouring Glen Affric were places full of memories. As we drove up the side of Loch Duich heading east to Glen Shiel and the starting point of my run, I recalled the last time I had been in and around this stretch of hills.

A few years before I'd travelled up one of Kintail's glens to cross a high bealach into Glen Affric. There's a remote youth hostel – Alltbeithe – high in Glen Affric that you have to make your own way to on foot or by bike. I had been cycling a Scottish Coast to Coast route from the Skye Bridge to Montrose in the east, over the far side of the Cairngorms, and stayed in the hostel for a night. To get there I'd ridden south-west from Morvich, close to the head of Loch Duich, up Glen Licht to Glenlicht House. From there the track turned to rougher path, I rode a little but mainly shouldered my bike up and over the pass and watershed at Camban, where one of the tributary burns that form the River Affric rises, which I followed the few miles down to the hostel.

Riding the Coast to Coast in mid-May 2010, it was a fine spring afternoon when I reached the high point at Camban. I stopped for a while, both for a breather and to let the scenery around me sink in a little more. From where I sat the view to the Five Sisters was sharp and stark – the sunlight casting shadows with the mountains' rugged and pointy shapes. I remember thinking about the texture of the landscape and the way this is influenced by light. Despite all my time in and around mountains prior to that moment, I think this may have been the first time I consciously acknowledged how light has such an influence on a landscape. This was about a year before I started painting mountains and, along with the intense moment of looking to the Flowerdale hills, this scene and experience was one of the seeds of this desire.

We parked at my starting point and as I left the car, I looked up to the hills. A layer of grey cloud hung about them so I couldn't see very high, about 400 metres. A muggy morning. While I had full waterproofs with me, I didn't think I'd need them and expected the cloud to soon burn off.

I didn't really think there would be an inversion – when you climb above the clouds to blue sky and sunshine – until I'd climbed up closer to the ridge. Aidan had dropped me about halfway up Glen Shiel, below Bealach an Làpan, a saddle point in the north Kintail ridge. My plan was to follow the path as it zigzagged the steep mountainside to reach the bealach and then follow the ridge west to traverse the Five Sisters.

Given the gradient, after leaving my drop-off point I soon gained height. Wearing a T-shirt and shorts and carrying a small pack with essentials, despite the layer of cloud it was warm and sweat was soon pouring off me.

There was a strange double layer to the cloud – at around 400 metres I passed through one layer to see the next around the same height again above me. The cloud just hung there, immobile, feeling static, not like the normal misty wisps that waft around mountains.

As I approached the ridge it became lighter above. This was when I got really excited about what it meant. I'd seen cloud inversions before back home from the top of the Otley Chevin and in the Lake District, but only once before in the Highlands.

They happen in a valley when colder air becomes trapped below warmer air above. Clouds condense below the warm air and form a flat layer that from above looks like a grey-white sea. When inversions form in the mountains some higher points typically remain above them, islands in a cloud-sea.

Clearing the mist I gasped aloud. Above me was blue sky, the sun shining warmly. The low point on the ridge I'd reached stood just clear of the mist below. All around me was the sea of clouds, the ridge and surrounding summits – the high-points of the Cluanie Ridge, Glen Affric, Knoydart, Mullardoch and more – were there to see, dark, shadowed peaks in the strong sunlight.

There was no noise, a calm was about this place, it was windless and still. I just stood and stared, marvelling at the beauty, thanking my lucky stars for being there that morning.

Like the scaly back of some enormous sea monster, the Five Sisters stretched out in front of me. In my dream-like state above the clouds I began to reimagine their story. Perhaps that's what the original five sisters actually became when they metamorphosed – a creature that only comes into being in these uncommon conditions, lying in wait to capture unsuspecting hill-goers. That seemed more fitting to me, instead of mournfully waiting centuries for some men to arrive, they could occasionally eat a few. As I started to run along her back, I was hoping my gender meant I would avoid this fate.

The ridgeline meandered, initially due west, and then north-west towards Sgùrr Fhuaran, the highest of the Five Sisters. The first of the five peaks I came to was Sgùrr nan Spainteach, followed by Sgùrr na Ciste Duibhe. As I reached this high point the mountains of Skye became visible. Also poking out of a sea of cloud, there was Blà Bheinn and the Black Cuillin, the smoother Red Cuillin nestled below and between them. The sharp dark crest of the Black Cuillin rose above the cloud like some crazy set of shark fins. Looking to them (and not really wishing I was anywhere else but where I was on the Five Sisters that morning),

I could also imagine the feeling of being on the Cuillin Ridge. I wanted to return to them soon. Aidan and I had traversed about half the ridge, its eastern end, about two years before. We wanted to go back to it at some point, to pick up our journey along it together.

Over my left shoulder to the south, Knoydart's mountains were in the background, the Saddle and Forcan Ridge on the other side of Glen Shiel before them. Like the Cuillin these were island-peaks. The air above the cloud had such clarity I could see the crags and other rock features of these mountains, grey and in shadow against the greens of the surrounding turf. The same was true when I looked in the other direction. The peaks of Glen Affric, Mullardoch, and beyond them Glen Carron, were dark shapes above the whiteness below.

Underfoot the terrain was smooth path in places and rocky in others. While my pace along the ridge was governed by this, I was in no hurry. I jogged along, walking at times simply to slow myself down and extend this morning run. I followed the path, heading more or less due north towards Sgùrr na Càrnach and then the pyramidal Sgùrr Fhuaran, the highest of the five summits. The inversion was as defined as ever; it felt kind of weird that I had almost got used to it, taking the beauty for granted. I knew as soon as I left the ridge it would change for me, that I would be unlikely to catch such conditions in the mountains for a long time.

As I traversed the ridge I saw no one. While in one way it would have been nice to have someone to pass the time of day with, to collectively marvel at what was before us, I think it would also have burst the dream-like bubble my head was in. Encouraged by the meditative rhythm of my running, up there I felt distanced from the world below by that cloud-sea.

The final peak of the Five Sisters, Sgùrr na Moraich, is an outlier. The main path ignores it, instead taking a south-west line that follows the Allt a'Chruinn burn off the ridge and down to the head of Loch Duich. I wanted to complete the ridge proper so I climbed Sgùrr na Moraich out and back, following the rough path to the summit.

My morning's journey was coming to an end, something I did not want to happen too quickly. On reaching this westernmost Sister, I sat down next to her cairn and let it all sink in some more. If she was a sea-monster, she was kind enough to let me do this without trying to eat me. After ten minutes or so I regretfully retraced my steps to the main path by the burn that would take me down, away from this dream world and back through the grey-white cloud to reality.

8. The Cuillin Ridge

Landscape of mineral

My climbing harness brought back memories of the days when all I did was climb, as did the exposure all about me as I steadily moved up the rocky crest that led to the summit of the Inaccessible Pinnacle. In front of me and to my back were Skye's dark, jagged Black Cuillin. Late afternoon with warm sun and a light breeze, it was a fine day to be up there, following the line of the ridge, negotiating and enjoying the scrambles and roped pitches along the way. Aidan and I were climbing together and it was my lead.

It was the day after my trip above the clouds along the Five Sisters of Kintail. Aidan's parents were babysitting and the two of us had started early, wanting to make the most of the time we had before us. From where we were staying in Kintail alongside Loch Long, we headed west over the Skye Bridge, through Broadford and Sligachan, and parked up next to the campsite in Glen Brittle. A warm day in July during a period of settled weather. Perfect for the Cuillin.

Our first time on the ridge had been two years before. Now, with aspirations to traverse the whole of the ridge in one trip (with a bivvy up high), after a mostly warm and dry first day, we were thwarted by thunderstorms, retreating off back to Glen Brittle.

It was only a couple of years since I had started painting. I found I was increasingly looking at mountains more intensely, becoming consciously aware of light and thinking about how this changes their look and mood. It took me much longer to realise that this mood is what I seek to capture in painting; at the time I just knew I wanted to look more than before.

The Black Cuillin are binary in their beauty, a harsh, jagged kind, monochrome, austere. A chain of high peaks connected by a rock ridge that frequently can be described as knife-edge, the main line crest of the ridge bends and twists, with other lines branching off. During my first time on it, looking along north from Sgùrr nan Eag at its southern end, the ridge felt both layered and daunting. A landscape of mineral, a classic and obvious mountain journey, a long way to successfully route-find and climb.

The rock itself is volcanic gabbro, dark and rough with high levels of friction. Among the sixteen peaks along the ridge are eleven Munros – a bagger's and rock-climber's paradise.

One day I will come and traverse this ridge in one go. But not as fast as I can. I may run bits but steady away, deliberately taking my time, letting it all sink in, sleeping in one of the sheltered spots dotted along its way. Before then I am content to climb it in portions, and ideally with Aidan. We have a sort of pact that neither will finish our staggered traverse before the other, that we will do it together. Given our current rate of progress, I think this will most likely happen with our two children (as teenagers) along for the ride.

Back to that July morning, when we planned to pick up the ridge where we had left off, conveniently, on the other side of the Thearlaich Dubh Gap. The TD Gap is a renowned, infamous even, rock climb on the line of the ridge. While experienced rock climbers will whistle across, it is limiting for others because it is a Severe graded climb and in damp conditions the rock is ice-like in its slippiness.

In my late teens and early twenties, rock-climbing had been my main pastime, my earliest outdoor obsession, and through it Aidan and I met. I had climbed throughout the UK, on moorland outcrops, mountain crags, sea-cliffs and quarries. He grew up in Sheffield, climbing on the gritstone edges of the eastern Peak District. So we were both experienced rock climbers, but back in our pasts. Neither of us had really climbed at the sharp end for well over a decade. While missing out the TD Gap in our broken traverse in some ways felt like cheating ourselves, it was also a relief.

From Glen Brittle we headed to Coire Lagan on a good path past the Eas Mòr falls, eastwards into the mountains. After steady climbing, the path steepened and soon enough we were standing next to Loch Coire Lagan, its dark water reflecting the grey buttresses rising up above it. A striking amphitheatre of rock, Coire Lagan is a destination in itself. From its opening at the lochan, steep gabbro climbs up and away, towards the summits and the ridge above. I felt an atmosphere of quiet and calm, but for the occasional, echoing sound of scree skittering down the Great Stone Chute.

The Great Stone Chute is one of the access points to the ridge, and it was this we would use to reach a small bealach to the immediate east of Sgùrr Alasdair. Its name is fitting – at its bottom a wide and steep scree slope, narrowing with height as it rises up to meet the ridge, looking lose all the way. There was something of a trail leading in zigzags up it. Like the scree, this path looked transient, likely to shift and fall away at any point.

Some people love scree running; I never have. Letting go in descent, moving fast and with the shifting rocks, stones and grit beneath your feet to me just feels destructive. That and my shoes fill with gravel, which I find really annoying. I resolved to just get on with climbing up to the bealach, my dislike and nervousness enhanced by someone directly above us carelessly knocking rocks down the chute. I put my climbing helmet on.

On reaching the ridge I immediately became less grumpy. The high line unfolded north ahead of us, snaking in its sharp and pointy way. Looking east to the other side of the ridge, I could see the blue water of Loch Coruisk and the smaller, but still jagged dark peaks, beyond it. All well worth the discomfort of the Great Stone Chute.

The predominant material is rock. That may read as an obvious statement, but aside from the ridges of Arran, the Black Cuillin are mountains unlike others in the UK, akin to the Alps and other higher mountains. In the world's major mountain ranges, it is above the tree line that the land becomes moraine, higher still rock. The Black Cuillin does this at the lowly height of 600 metres.

As I gazed out, over and along the ridge, someone else's words sprang into my mind...

**Sgurr Alisdair the highest sgurr
but Sgurr nan Gillean the best sgurr,
the black-blue gape-mouthed strong sgurr,
the sapling, slender, horned sgurr,
the forbidding, great, dangerous sgurr,
the sgurr of Skye above all other sgurrs.**

*Sgùrr Alasdair an sgùrr as àirde
ach Sgùrr nan Gillean sgùrr an àigh dbiubh,
an sgùrr grom-dhubh, craosach, làidir,
an sgùrr gallanach, caol, cracach,
an sgùrr iargalta, mòr, gàbhaidg,
an sgùrr Sgitheanach thar chàich dhiubh*

At the time I'd been reading about the Cuillin and not through route and climbing guides but poetry. In my wider explorations of other people's mountain stories, in particular those telling of the Scottish Highlands and Islands, I had just found my way to the words of Sorley MacLean and his poem *An Cuilithionn*.

A poet and teacher who was born in 1911 on Raasay, a small island off the coast of Skye, MacLean has become recognised as one of the (if not *the*) pre-eminent modern Gaelic poets. He mostly translated his poems to English himself. In each of the books of his poetry I have, the Gaelic and English versions sit on opposite pages, line by line they flow together. While I may not be able to understand the Gaelic, I can appreciate its texture and richness. More than anything it is through the reading of MacLean's poems in this way I have come to appreciate the importance of Gaelic to the culture and memory of the Highlands and Islands. It is the physical, emotional and social language of the land.

The poem itself is an epic. Within it MacLean uses the Cuillin symbolically, they represent revolution. He describes the physical richness of these mountains and their surrounding land vividly, using their strength, beauty and form as a metaphor for many, at times, opposing things, including oppressed people, their oppressors, corruption and the strength of the human spirit.

MacLean died in 1996, leaving a large body of work, the importance of which it seems is still in the process of being fully recognised. I am no poetry scholar, but in the years since I first read his words I have gone back to them again and again. He wrote love poetry, poetry of place, of his culture, his people's history. The Clearances feature, of course. 'Hallaig', likely his most famous poem, tells of the empty and ruined township of Hallaig on Raasay, now populated by the ghosts of his people. He also writes much of the clans of the Highlands and Islands, local groups of people sharing the kinships of history, ancestry, geography and place.

Throughout it all there is a strong sense that MacLean completely understood the power of words to reclaim, remember and reinvigorate. That he did it all with such style and beauty was his genius.

As I stood on the ridge above the Great Stone Chute that July morning, I had a few of Sorley MacLean's descriptions of the place whirling around inside my head. At the time I did not know much about the man or just how much of his poetry I would explore, but his words had clearly already affected me.

Before we headed north along the ridge we went south to reach the summit of Sgùrr Alisdair, the highest peak on the Cuillin and all the mountains of Skye. From the little bealach at the top of the stone chute we did not have far to climb – it is steep up to this pyramidal peak, which is so pointed that we just about had enough space for the two of us to stand next to the small cairn that marks the summit.

After that we doubled back, descending back to the bealach and then continuing our intermittent traverse of the ridge. The next summit we would reach was Sgùrr Mhic Choinnich, but before that we needed to negotiate the King's Chimney. Albeit relatively easy (VDiff), this is route we would rope up for and climb wearing harnesses, using pieces of my aged climbing rack for protection. This was a collection of rocks, karabiners and slings that had been sitting in a box for years in our garage. Before coming to the Cuillin we had gone through our old gear, deciding on a set of kit we would likely need and leaving the rest behind so we could move lightweight. While we maybe should not having been using such old equipment, we had to admit that we needed to buy a new rope.

We had agreed I would lead, so on reaching the foot of the chimney, I pulled the rack out of my pack, put my harness on and readied myself to climb. Aidan brought our rope out of his pack and started to uncoil it at our feet.

Unsurprisingly the rock of the chimney is polished, edges worn by the passage of many feet. Looking up I could see the line was pretty straightforward; I just needed to get on with it. Moving up I wedged a wire in a crack, clipped in and felt a little more secure. Familiar feelings of excitement and nervousness I had not experienced for nearly two decades began to fill me.

Soon enough I got to the crux – the hardest move. All I had to do was step to the right, out from the chimney, onto what looked like small but positive edges for my feet, reach up for a handhold, which itself would put me within easy reach of the ledge that marked the top of the route and the end of the roped climb. Easy to look at, to decipher and to write about, I found it hard to commit to the move. I wished I was wearing my sticky rubber climbing shoes, but we'd left them behind to save weight.

Only when a queue of others traversing the ridge began to form behind us did I make the move. Two men standing next to Aidan seemed patient enough, but I didn't want to hold them and others up. This new pressure forced my head to get on with it, compelling me to step out and across. As I had thought, it was straightforward enough even in trainers, I was soon sitting on the ledge, smiling, making a belay and bringing Aidan up.

When we reached the summit of Sgùrr Mhic Choinnich, we received an apology from the guy who had accidently knocked rocks down towards us as we climbed the Great Stone Chute. After talking some more, he told us he was about halfway through a journey to climb all the Munros in one go. Little wonder he had such a big smile on his face; probably in his early twenties, he was living his dream and it was evident in his enthusiasm and conversation. Here he was in the middle of it, that day climbing some of the most iconic of mountains. He told us he'd worked the winter in Glasgow, saving up enough to fund this three-month adventure in the Highlands. I felt both envious and impressed. The left sole of his knackered walking boots was flapping loose but that did not seem to slow him down and he left us, running, heading like us towards the Inaccessible Pinnacle.

The Inaccessible Pinnacle is unique among the Munros in that it is the only summit that requires a rock climb. Typically climbed up its western or eastern ridges with an abseil descent, to reach the summit requires rock-climbing experience or a guide who can show the way.

As we left Sgùrr Mhic Choinnich heading towards this climb, I wondered how many people who approached the Inaccessible Pinnacle were like Aidan and me. Serious climbers into our mid-twenties who, for one reason or other, hadn't climbed in anger for years. Now approaching middle-age, the Munro-baggers in us needed to climb the Inaccessible Pinnacle and the climbers in us wanted to relive past times.

The Pinnacle loomed ahead of us as we approached along the dusty path. A squat looking sentinel standing proud on the ridge, while it didn't look all that scary and was an easier climb than the King's Chimney, I again had that familiar nervous trepidation rising in me.

One thing I was quite determined about was not to get in a queue. Back in my climbing days, experiences of long waits on popular mountain rock-climbing pitches in the Lakes and Alps as others faffed up ahead, combined by a seemingly hard-wired need to always move fast and light in the mountains, led me to want to stay ahead. I was, therefore, disheartened to see a pair in front of us, trying to uncoil their own rope at the foot of the Inaccessible

Pinnacle. I say 'trying to' as the man was making a meal of it, looking like it was going to take him ages to run it through.

Aidan and I approached the bottom of the east ridge of the pinnacle, taking our own rope, harnesses and climbing rack out of our packs to ready ourselves for the route. Standing close to the other two, we shared smiles and soon enough started talking. They were called Brian and Jane. Brian hadn't climbed in anger for over twenty-five years and was looking a bit apprehensive. Jane had never climbed. Brian had promised her the help she needed to get to the summit of the Inaccessible Pinnacle.

Soon afterwards the all-in-a-oner Munro guy reappeared (I never did catch his name), this time with a friend. She was from Portland, Oregon, and was cycle-touring around Europe. The two of them had met down in the Glen Brittle campsite and she had agreed to hold his ropes on the Inaccessible Pinnacle. Wearing flip-flops and looking incredibly chilled, she looked a relaxed and very cool person to be sharing a rope with.

There we were, the six of us. To start with I had wanted to (politely) push in front of Brian and Jane – it would make sense as we would clearly move faster than them and be out of their way in no time – ahead of us they would just be a bottleneck. This was my speed conscious climber and racer-head speaking and it annoyed Aidan. He quietly and firmly told me we would wait our turn. Once he'd said this my mindset changed. Instead of wanting to be in a hurry I realised that there was no need to try to move all that fast, I could actually slow down, chat to the others, enjoy the view.

What followed was a lovely spell of the six of us all enjoying our climbs up the pinnacle. Aidan talked more to the guys behind us and I more with Jane, as Brian climbed ahead. As Brian finished the first pitch, Jane began climbing. After a while I followed and, as I approached Jane, with Brian finishing the second pitch, I found myself advising her on how strip her belay and start climbing again.

The eastern ridge is straightforward to climb but exposed, with sheer drops on both sides of me. I used to be so familiar with the feelings that come with rock climbing in high places, to have them again felt both new and old. With a backdrop of the Black Cuillin all around me, I moved steadily upwards, my mind quietly blown by the feelings of where I was, what I was doing, and what I could see.

Approaching the summit, Aidan moved through and then brought me up on belay. While doing this he was also advising Brian and Jane how to run their rope through the metal chain close to the summit in order to abseil off. We later laughed at the fact that both of us had been sharing advice on these things given we hadn't climbed rock routes in anger or abseiled an approach or descent for well over a decade.

After they finished their abseil we ran our own rope through the abseil chain and followed. Memories of abseils I had made in the Alps, UK sea cliffs and mountain crags in North Wales and the Lakes came back to me. Despite the years since I'd last descended in this way, the methodical process of doing it safely was still imprinted in my mind. The prussic loop I wrapped around the rope from the leg loop of my harness would protect me in the event my hands came away from the rope as I descended. I moved smoothly down the rope, pushing my feet against the rock wall to help maintain control of my movement.

On reaching the ground of the ridge once more we coiled the rope, took off our helmets and harnesses and packed them away. Sitting around on the rocks for a while, we waited for the two guys following us to finish their abseil and just generally hung around, enjoying the place and the late afternoon sun. You could feel the happiness and satisfaction brimming up in the six of us. Whether or not you go in for Munro-bagging, the Inaccessible Pinnacle is one of the iconic Scottish summits. Requiring more than walking to get to it instils nervousness in many. It wasn't that we had conquered this peak, more that we'd enjoyed the shared adventure that climbing it had been.

After a little while we said our goodbyes and started to make our way back down towards Glen Brittle, wistfully casting our eyes further along the ridge to the part that neither of us had yet traversed. We were leaving it behind for another blue moon day, when we could come back and finish the ridge together.

And this particular blue moon day wasn't yet over. The line of our descent took us back through the solid rock of Coire Lagan. The gabbro had such incredible friction I found I could descend steep slabs with little concern about slipping or falling. It was getting late; the sun cast long shadows in the coire, surrounded by the amphitheatre of solid dark grey.

At the entrance to the coire we had a clear view to the Isle of Eigg, beyond it Ardnamurchan and, further still, Mull's Ben More stood proud, silhouetted in light blue against the sky and sea. We steadily descended the path back to Glen Brittle, my head spinning from this day on the hill, not really wanting it to end.

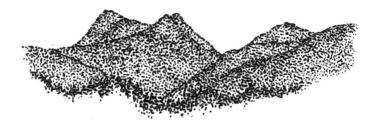

9. Glen Strontian
Beneath Sgùrr Dhomhnull

Four months after our second daughter was born, the four of us embarked on a four-week trip to the Highlands and Islands. Late summer and a month before the eldest of our two children started primary school, we wanted to get away for a longer family trip. Starting with Arran, then Islay, Mull and Strontian in Sunart, we would spend a week in each place. This would be a trip up the south-west coast, exploring again places we had been before as well as visiting parts of the Highlands new to us.

It was a month of moving slower, at the pace of a four-year-old with a four-month-old strapped close to me in a sling on my front. It felt like a month of looking at views, because, while I could get away for an hour or so, this was generally not long enough to get up and down a mountain. I found myself planning to get away for a few hours, expressing enough milk so I could do so, then realising I couldn't bring myself to leave Robyn for that long anyway.

During our time on Arran, Aidan went for a few long runs over the mountains. Each time the girls and I met him at a different point to where he had started so he could have a more interesting, linear run. While I didn't begrudge him these, I was jealous. We'd previously spent time together on the ridges and peaks of Arran so I know how fine they are. I also knew this frustration would be relatively short-lived, that opportunities for long mountains runs would come back to me; I just needed to relax and be patient.

After a week of wet and windy weather on Islay we returned to Mull for our first visit since Aidan and I kayaked to Staffa. I got to climb Ben More again. It must be one of the most straightforward of the Munros, at least on the most commonly used route from Loch na Keal. I ran up and down between breastfeeds, basking in the view from the summit and the feelings of freedom that came with it.

If having children makes you less selfish, it also makes you more patient. I'll be honest and say I have found the decreased freedom to head into the mountains something hard to reconcile. However, this is not something I dwell on and I also know it is a transient thing. I am sure that before I know it, in the years to come when this becomes easier again, I will miss the days I am living now and at times yearn to return to them. Living in and enjoying the moment, where things are at right now, is one of the routes to a greater degree of happiness and contentment. My children have taught me this.

Being with them, moving more slowly has also helped me to learn something important. At a slower pace you see more, both in the artistic sense and in spending time looking at things differently. I also see things through their eyes, as they ask questions of and comment on the things we see and visit. What a wealth of freshness, unimpeded by the pressures of expectation and perceived normality.

When we were on Mull we returned to the beach close to Ffionport, where Aidan and I had camped and kayaked about eight years before. An afternoon of beachcombing, cowrie shell collecting and kite-flying ensued. At home I have a glass jar half-full of cowrie shells I'd found on the beaches of South and

North Uist during my first visit to them when I was eighteen. This little jar and its contents has clearly meant something to me – as I kept it as an ornament in my room while at university and then afterwards, in all the different houses I have lived in through the years. It is my memories of the Outer Hebrides. I hadn't hunted for shells in all that time, but it is something I love to do. While in my view it is cowrie shells that are the real treasures, I also love the lilac shells with spirals that finish in a point, and small pieces of broken sea anemones, found in regular square and rectangular shapes, full of rich purples and crimsons with white dots standing proud.

Together with Alanna, I found a few new cowrie shells to add to the jar when we got back home to Yorkshire. In the four years since then we've occasionally added to the jar again, after other trips to the west coast and islands. Whether I like it or not, what started as my own collection is now shared.

After our time spent beachcombing I fancied a cup of tea; Aidan and Alanna wanted cake. We began the slow drive along the winding roads of western Mull back to where we were staying, keeping an eye out for somewhere we could get a brew.

We didn't have to go far. Shortly after leaving Ffionport we saw a sign for The Eco-Croft, which promised tea and cake. Following the dead-end road we arrived after a mile or so. The door was open and we walked into small shop selling local produce – meat, along with fruit and vegetables grown in the market garden out the back of the croft in a sheltered area between two rocky knolls. In the corner of the shop were a couple of tables and chairs, alongside everything needed to make a cup of tea or coffee and some slices of home-made cakes on a cake stand. Running on an honesty system, a small sign asked us to record whatever we brought in a little book on the side and to leave cash for them in the kitty.

Putting the kettle on and bickering about who was going to get which cake, we sat down for a while, Robyn sitting on my lap looking around as four-month-olds do. In the corner of the room a shelf full of wool caught my eye. After finishing my tea I went over to take a look. Different shades of browns and creams, spun from the fleece of local Jacob sheep. There were kits to make a pair of gloves and also a hat. Each came with enough wool, the needles required and instructions. I decided to buy one of each. Aidan rolled his eyes at me as if to say 'Seriously? Knitting?' Yes.

When I was younger, into my late teens, I did loads of crafts. Jewellery making, bead-weaving, mosaics made from stone and shells. I was always feeling inspired to try to make something, spending my pocket money on materials and scavenging other bits. When I went off to university to study maths, I also began rock climbing and fell running in earnest and that was it really, I left it all behind. In that little croft on Mull I felt it all coming back.

That evening, back in the cottage we were staying in close to Salen, I found a YouTube video that showed me how to cast on and I was off, beginning my first glove, a simple rectangle of knitting that I would stitch together to form a fingerless mitten. The wool was soft and thick, knitting into a warm material. Within a few days I had finished the gloves and before the end of our trip I'd started on the hat, this time knitting in a circle, 'in the round'.

From Mull we moved to Strontian, the last place we would stay during this month. It's a short ride on the little ferry from Fishnish that connects the north of the island to the Movern region of the Highlands, west of Loch Linne, on the far side of this water from Glencoe. Strontian is in Sunart, just north of Morvern, in neighbouring Ardnamurchan. Off the main routes around the Highlands, these are quieter places that neither Aidan or I had visited before but had meant to for years. We were looking forward to exploring and learning more about them.

The cottage we stayed in had a view up Glen Strontian. From a wide window we could see out over the forests to the open mountainside, to the summit of Sgùrr Dhomhnull towering over the glen. Through the week I would sit there all hours, feeding Robyn, sometimes knitting or reading, occasionally looking up to gaze up at the mountain. In the early mornings in particular this was the perfect frame for the mountain. The light mist lingering about its higher reaches, tempting me to climb it in this clear cool air of early autumn.

Writing these words I still have that picture of the mountain in my mind. It still lures me back and I want to go and climb it with Aidan and our children, to explore the old lead mines on the hillside along the way. I've promised them sunshine and picnics; they seem pretty keen. Back then I had mixed feelings – while it was lovely to sit there and look up to the mountain, I could not suppress the irrepressible urge I had to climb it, all in all the feelings were bittersweet.

While in itself I find knitting relaxing, calming for my busy mind and it's great to wear the jumpers and other things I've made (when they fit), it means more to me than that. Knitting, and thinking about knitting, puts me in touch with the old ways of doing, makes me think about how craft and 'making' relates to the land, the place. While mountains are an important part of the culture in the Highlands and Islands, it is the land surrounding them that tells the stories of the people that lived there, before the Clearances drove so many of them away.

In past times, the rearing and shearing of sheep, followed by spinning and knitting the wool was a fundamental part of ensuring people had warm clothing. Furthermore, the very act of knitting was one of the means of preserving a culture. The talking, gossiping and storytelling that went on as groups of people knitted together, passing on methods to each other, keeping the old skills and tales alive.

The patterns and designs are themselves often very local – all around the UK coast for example, the patterns of fishermen's ganseys are specific to where they lived. In practical (and sad) terms, this meant those who died at sea and whose bodies were recovered, could be more easily identified. Many knitting designs are also abstractions of the land around the knitter. Art and place knitted into a thing of beauty and utility – one of the reasons the colourful and intricate Fair Isle patterns came to be is because knitting a jumper with more than one yarn at once makes it thicker, warmer and less permeable to water.

In exploring culture of the Highlands and Islands, I began to read and explore the history more than I ever had. Doing so made them became more than places of physical beauty and challenge. I am coming to appreciate and value them even more deeply, and this is growing as I further read and learn.

It is with a sense of envy that I watch the Scots – the peoples of the Highlands and Islands – remembering their history and culture more widely and reclaiming their heritage. A heritage connected to landscapes of beauty, harsh landscapes within which survival was tough; the crafts they needed to survive intertwined with storytelling to form collective memory – a cultural history. Something that on one hand is honed from supreme practicality, on the other made up of artefacts and stories of intense creativity.

This history and culture is, of course, being reclaimed from the people who took it from them through assimilation. The age-old process of taking through force and ruling by decree, ensuring the local people forget by outlawing their religions, languages, ways of doing and of being. There is a sense of shame in being English. I feel it. I also feel a sense of sadness, anger even, at the ways down the years the perpetrators of these assimilation processes have been able to claim England's cultural history.

I've been thinking about this for a while now but instead of dwelling on the ill-feeling, I have started to look beyond it. The fascinating thing is that the stories of knitting can take you there. Other crafts too. I have found a thrill in learning some of the old ways, remembering them through reading and doing. Remembering reclaims things. It's a form of rebellion.

And I also know I have the tingling feeling I get in the woods above my house in Yorkshire on a dark afternoon in midwinter. They can't take that from me. Herne the Hunter, the Green Man, Mother Earth herself. My culture goes further back than a red cross on a white background. It's telling that time spent in Scotland, thinking about and exploring the history of the Highlands and Islands, helped me to realise this.

During our time in staying in Strontian we explored, travelled out to and explored Ardnamurchan, played on the beach at Sanna, climbed its famous lighthouse and met the old lighthouse keeper at the top who was its guide. We walked along the edge of Loch Sunart, watching eiders and divers on the water. In the evenings I would head out on my bike for an hour or so, sometimes climbing up to the road pass close to Druim Glas, where I would get a view over the hills and watch them change with the lowering evening sunlight.

A few times we walked in the ancient oakwood in the glen below Sgùrr Dhomhnull, down which the River Strontian flows. Ariundle Oakwood or Airigh Fhionndail, meaning 'the shieling of the white meadow', is a nature reserve and one of the few remnants of the oak woods that used to line the whole of the western seaboard of the British Isles. Even though it was generally raining with the dull light that comes with such weather, the place was still full of colour and vibrant with life. Lichens of intense sea-greens, oak leaves edging towards their autumn yellows and golds and the fluffy, rusty delight of the occasional red squirrel. To Alanna they were Nutkin himself jumping through the trees. We heard and saw a gang of long-tailed tits, a jay with an acorn in its beak, watched a treecreeper climbing the bark of an oak tree, and tried hard (and in vain) to spot the goldcrest, whose high-pitched call we could hear in the canopy above our heads.

I felt like we'd spent our stay in Strontian in the shadow of a mountain, exploring more deeply what lies beneath. I took away with me a sense of peace, and also strong desire to return, to climb Sgùrr Dhomhnull, and more widely to explore the hills of Ardgour and neighbouring Morven, Moidart and Sunart. These are quiet mountains, overlooked and left alone by Munro-baggers as there are none to bag. And they are beautiful.

10. Ladhar Bheinn
A fresh pair of antlers

As I started to descend from the summit of Beinn Sgritheall, the light to the south-east suddenly changed. Initially I fumbled with my camera, then stopped running and stood still, determined to capture the look of the landscape in front of me before it changed again. Immediately I knew that this scene would become a painting and could already picture myself back home in Yorkshire standing at my easel, working from this photograph. This time spent painting would bring back my time on the mountain above Arnisdale on this remote part of the west coast of the Highlands, close to where Gavin Maxwell wrote *Ring of Bright Water* and the old Skye ferry crossing at Glenelg.

The end of July 2018 and a prolonged spell of hot dry weather had broken just in time for our holiday to Kintail. I was initially disappointed until I realised what it meant for the look of the mountains. Throughout our week staying at foot of the western end of the Five Sisters by Kintail Bridge, I saw them in many different kinds of light created by the heavy dark clouds that carry rain and the sun's intermittent rays breaking through. Something you don't get in the unending sun of a heatwave.

The Highland region I was looking into as I descended Beinn Sgritheall was Knoydart. Towering over Loch Hourn, Ladhar Bhienn, the largest of these hills, was the peak that had most captured my imagination. While there was sunlight on this mountain and the loch in front of it, other close-by ridges and tops were in darkness. Combined with the heavy, dark clouds above the scene was compelling. I wanted to both be in it and to paint it. As I ran down the mountain, I began to hatch a plan for how both Aidan and I could together head into Knoydart for another visit.

We'd been there together before in the spring of 2007 and walked to Barrisdale Bay from Kinlochhorn. A bright, warm day in March not long after fresh snow, the mountain tops were white and there were fast-thawing patches among the browns of the lower ground we travelled across. The air was clear and the light soft, the scenery around us compelling. I had wanted to stay longer, to experience more of this place. On that short trip, however, we stayed low, looking to the hills instead of climbing them, leaving with strong desire to return.

Over a decade after that spring walk into the edge of Knoydart, a year after my gazing to Ladhar Bheinn from the mountainside above Arnisdale, I finally had a plan to return. The following summer we booked a cottage on Loch Morar, south of the Knoydart hills, close to Mallaig, staying with our children and Aidan's parents. Aidan and I hoped to head into Knoydart together via the ferry from Mallaig to Inverie and camp high in the hills before returning to our family the following morning.

This was foiled as Aidan ended up having a bad cold for most of the week, not up to hill walking. We agreed instead that I would catch the boat by myself for the day. On the early ferry, I would take my bike, climb Ladhar Bhienn and another hill or two and hopefully have enough time for a pint in The Old Forge before returning on the late afternoon boat out of Inverie.

Inverie is famed for being the most remote village on the UK mainland. Inaccessible by road, the main way into and out of it is by a small passenger ferry from Maillaig. This boat also serves as Inverie's main connection point with the rest of the world in other ways, collecting and delivering the post as well as provisions for the shop and other necessities.

The village sits on the northern shore of Loch Nevis and is one of the most commonly used access points into Knoydart. Though small, it has a bunkhouse, pub and a little shop. The pub, The Old Forge, is famous for being the most remote pub on the UK mainland.

Mid-August in the Highlands meant the stag hunting season was well under way. As I planned my trip I tried in vain to determine whether I would be restricted in the hills I hoped to climb, because of the risk of stalking activity. After searching online I found a phone number, hoping for the promised answerphone message to provide this information. Nothing. What to do? I decided to go anyway, and to be prepared to change my planned run if required.

Early the following morning I left the cottage and cycled the seven or so miles to Maillaig. Waiting for the ferry in the harbour I watched the water for fish. Two nights before, with Aidan and Alanna, I had first tried my hand at mackerel fishing. The night before that we'd seen that the fish had been jumping from the water. Coming back with a rod and lure the following evening, Alanna caught three mackerel with her first cast. It didn't take us long at all before we'd caught six, enough for our dinner so we called it an evening, returning to the cottage to cook and eat them. In our excitement and taste for the fish we had returned the day after, only to prove to ourselves that the previous evening had been beginner's luck as we caught nothing.

There were just a few other people on the early ferry. I noticed a man dressed in tweeds like a ghillie, suggesting he would be shooting somewhere close to Inverie. I asked him where the day's hunt would be, but he professed ignorance, saying he would find out only after he'd arrived in Inverie and met up with his colleagues.

The boat powered across the water. I looked to the hills. Ladhar Bheinn set back to the north, some of the other mountains of Knoydart – Luinne Bheinn and Meall Buidhe – loomed up imposingly to the east. Given I knew a shoot was going to happen, but not where, I figured I had a choice: head to Ladhar Bheinn or Luinne Bheinn and Meall Buidhe. Assuming they wouldn't be hunting in both places that day (indeed they might not be hunting in either), one of these places would be quiet and free from people shooting their guns into the hills.

Given the fifty-fifty chance I decided to stay with my objective of Ladhar Bheinn. I planned to cycle to the foot of the mountain on tracks, leave my bike and climb the hill following the main footpath. I would then follow the south-east ridge in descent, continuing as this ridgeline turned south-west, along Aonach Sgoilte and up to the high point on the opposite side of the glen from Ladhar Bheinn. This would be my horseshoe and then I'd descend to my bike waiting for me somewhere in the heather.

Soon enough we arrived at the Inverie jetty. I immediately started riding the road that met the jetty. The first thing I noticed was the masses of midges. It seemed on this clear and still morning they were trying to make up for days of not being out with the rain and the wind. Moving faster by cycling helped keep them off.

Finding the beginning of the track that would take me to Ladhar Bheinn, I followed it and immediately began to climb steeply away from Inverie. After a few miles and a right turn a mile or so away from where I would leave my bike and start running, I saw a guy in a 4x4. Friendly and smiling, he told me they would be shooting there later, that I would be fine if I stayed to the path, to head up and back down the mountain the same way.

The track ended at a small copse of trees and a couple of shielings. I took off my cycle helmet and rested it in the heather next to my bike, looking around and reminding myself exactly where I was leaving it, I have almost lost bikes before in similar situations, hidden as they can be in the bogland.

Feeling controlled and annoyed (not with the man in the van, he was only doing his job), if my route had to be up and down the mountain the same way after all, so be it. I started up the path, which gradually steepened as I left the glen and gained height. My thoughts were clouded, a sense of not feeling free in the hills as I usually do and, despite what I had just been told about safety, an underlying worry that soon there would be people shooting their guns on the hill I was climbing. I resolved to focus on the scenery, which was fine to start with and improving even more as I gained height. When I reached the summit ridge I knew I would get an immense view out over Barrisdale Bay and the mountains beyond, a reverse of the scene from the previous summer and something I had been looking forward to.

The hills were green, rich and deep in the sunlight. A few wispy mist patches lingered around the summit, occasionally making the light hazy. The view from the summit was as I had hoped, the wild Rough Bounds of Knoydart spread out before me, tantalising, again making me want to both be in the scene and to paint it.

I had paper and pen with me and sat down with the aim of doing a quick sketch to try to capture the scene in the traditional, analogue, way rather than taking photographs with a digital camera as I usually do. This was all going well until the midges increasingly appeared, crawling around my head and biting. I pulled out my camera, took a few shots and then packed my stuff away and made to run off the hill, resolving to finish the sketch later.

As I descended I saw two more vehicles a way off, parked next to the copse close to where I'd left my bike. I started to worry about what that meant – despite being assured that in keeping to the path I would be safe from the shooting, it did not feel like a good thing. Acutely aware of the dull colours of my clothes, I wished I'd gone for something fluoro. About a third of the way down I passed two walkers heading up, which was a little reassuring. I stopped and mentioned the shoot. They were staying in Inverie and had also tried to find out where the shoot would happen that day in order to avoid it.

It was frustrating. I had wanted – and tried – to find a place in these hills where I could forget about everything else and indulge myself with mountains.

The landscape of Knoydart is a wonder and yet that day it felt fake. This is managed land and I was being managed – one of the very things I strive to get away from in coming to the hills. Shepherd the hill-goers into funnels, stop me running free. I could have still done the run I'd intended, but did not want the even greater nervousness, and the ghillies certainly did not want me off the beaten path on those hills.

I think I understand this. There is a conflict between hill-goers who want the freedom of the mountains and the hunting industry. This is supposed to be avoided by the hill phones system. I'd tried to find where the shoot would be, but it hadn't worked and meant I'd rubbed up against it.

The Highlands, at least in part, look as they do – our romantic concept of wild beauty – because they are managed for hunting. In the past there were far more trees; in the UK ancient forests are where the true wildness lies. Today there are far less than there used to be.

Two years or so after my trip into Knoydart, when I was close to writing these words, I read Edward Abbey's *Desert Solitaire*, first published in 1968.

A writer in and of the American West, his writing is underpinned by a love for wilderness lands – the Canyonlands – of the deserts of Utah and Arizona. Anarchic in style and attitude, as well as being a writer, he was an environmentalist and a seer. He knew what would increasingly happen to his beloved wilderness as the pressures of industry and tourism were brought to bear.

Abbey wrote of a few summers he spent working as a ranger in the Arches National Park. The book is made up of a flow of Abbey's desert stories, tales of his journeys, the landscape and the thinking inspired by them. The chapter 'Down the River' contains some of his most thoughtful and beautiful writing. He relates a week-long canoe trip down the Colorado, into the soon to be dammed Glen Canyon, an area of wilderness and Abbey was already mourning its loss in the name of industrial progress. When Abbey launches off down the river with his companion Ralph in their inflatable canoes, his immediate thoughts are reflections on how crazy modern life is and how, in the Western world, we choose to live.

My *God*! I'm thinking, what incredible *shit* we put up with for most of our lives... and what utterly *useless crap* we bury ourselves in day by day, while patiently enduring at the same time the creeping strangulation of the clean white *collar* and the rich but *modest* four-in-hand gavotte!

He goes on to discuss how this realisation of what modern life actually is becomes stark whenever he re-encounters the wilderness, and that it is the interests of the Establishment to ensure that this does not happen.

That's what the first taste of the wild does to a man, after having been too long penned up in the city. No wonder the authorities are so anxious to smother the wilderness under asphalt and reservoirs. They know what they're doing: their lives depend on it, and all their rotten institutions. Play safe. Ski only in a clockwise direction. Let's all have fun together.

Abbey believed that control is exerted over society by making us continually turn the hamster wheel, and that the disruption that could threaten this control is avoided by trying to ensure members of society don't get to see the wilder alternatives.

There is melancholy and a deep sadness underpinning Abbey's writing. He was hyper-aware that his adventure into Glen Canyon would be one of the last explorations of this kind before it would be flooded and was heading into this wilderness for one last, lingering look. Through his writing he shows us the place, its secrets and wonders. Desperation was in his voice (along with a dark, sardonic humour). He knew it would all soon be desecrated, submerged by a flooding he was powerless to stop.

In a beautifully written section of this chapter Abbey tells how, deep in the canyon, he explored Anasazi petroglyphs. The Anasazi lived in the Canyonlands around a thousand years ago; the petroglyphs were images they had made that were soon to be systematically submerged and destroyed by the damming of the river. Stories and signals from the old ones who had so much more knowledge of how to live in the balance with the Earth than we do today. I read with a feeling of desperation, a sadness at what we humans do regardless and mindlessly, unaware at what we're destroying until long after it's gone.

While it does not have the same expanse and remoteness as the wild areas of the Canyonlands of the American Southwest that Abbey adored, Knoydart is perceived to be one of the wildest parts of the UK. An extensive section of the Rough Bounds – the districts of Moidart, Arisaig, Morar and Knoydart, bordered by Loch Moidart and Loch Hourn to the south and north respectively – an area of the western Highlands renowned historically and today for its remoteness.

Knoydart is loved by many hill-goers, myself included, for this wildness. How much of this is due to romantic perceptions of the place I'm not sure, just as I'm not sure how much this matters. Abbey discusses this in 'Down the River', along with what a love for wild places means:

Suppose we say that wilderness invokes nostalgia, a
justified not merely sentimental nostalgia for the lost
America or forefathers knew. The word suggests the past
and the unknown, the womb of the earth from which we
all emerged. It means something lost and something still
present, something remote and at the same time intimate,
something buried in our blood and nerves, something
beyond us and without limit. Romance – but not to be
dismissed on that account. The romantic view, while not
the whole of truth, is a necessary part of the whole truth.

I held my romantic notions for Knoydart when I had gazed
across from Beinn Sgritheall the year before, and during the
ensuing year while I made plans for a journey into it with
Aidan. To assume that the wilderness will be there for me is a
presumption that maybe I don't deserve. The insidious creep of
destruction in the name of progress is everywhere; nearly all of
us play a part.

I followed a trod back towards the copse and found my bike
in the heather. Given the midges, I didn't hang around – soon
enough I was retracing my route to Inverie with air flowing past
me again, keeping the wee beasties away. My time on the hill
had been far shorter than I originally envisaged; I had plenty
of time for some food in the Old Forge. The place was quiet; if
there had been any kind of lunchtime rush, it was over. I treated
myself to prawns and a pint of bitter while spending some time
imagining the loud and lively evening ceilidhs.

After that I still had plenty of time before the next return ferry.
I wandered along the only road of the peninsula that runs
alongside the bay, passing a community shelter with a few
chairs and books near the community shop. A look inside the
shop revealed it was full of locally made arts and crafts. A perfect
place to buy a few presents for my family, in part because they
were very nice and the shop and shelter were splendid. I was
also having a fine day out and wanted to salve my guilt at having
this time all to myself in the hills.

There was another woman in the shop who looked as though she was doing something similar to me. She was served before me and told the woman behind the counter what a wonderful community spirit she'd encountered in the five days she had been there. Behind the counter the lady smiled, but you could sense she'd had that conversation hundreds of times before and when it came to my turn I said as much. We chatted about Ladhar Bheinn and my bike (she lusted after a gravel bike) and knew all about the Three Peaks Cyclo-Cross and Yorkshire Dales trails as she had lived there for a while.

We started to talk of Knoydart's community spirit. She told me the community was great, but that it takes forever to get over to do anything on the mainland. If, for example, she wants to go for a bike ride over there, she has to factor in both ferries and the limitations this brings. She also said she'd lived all over the UK and found that, while Inverie is a rural community, it's much like one she'd lived in in North Devon. She shared her feeling that the people who mainly commented to her about the community spirit were city people who thought that this was unique to Knoydart, not realising it could actually be found somewhat closer to them – all they had to do was head out to the countryside.

I packed my presents in my rucksack and went out to sit in the shelter and read, waiting for the ferry. After a while I pulled paper and pen from my saddlebag and started to sketch again. Shortly after this I was troubled by wasps. Combined with the midges at the top of the mountain, insects were clearly against me doing art outdoors that day.

I wandered along to the jetty, wheeling my bike. It was getting to be time for the ferry. The woman who had been ahead of me in the shop was waiting, along with another party of about eight people. They had all been staying for at least a few days, judging by all the bags they had with them. One of the party spoke with a strong Scottish accent and was fully dressed in a kilt with sporran and a matching jacket. The rest of his party were dressed in a pretty standard way.

An outsider looking in, I watched them. Where were they from? Was this their annual pilgrimage to a place of their heritage – it certainly seemed important to the man in the kilt, who had strapped a fresh pair of antlers to the outside of his rucksack and was proudly carrying them around. Over the years, having made many false assumptions and ignorant generalisations, I try not to go with first impressions, but this one screamed stereotype.

The roots of the antlers were still red with blood. I wondered if he would ever eat the meat of the stag whose antlers he had claimed, or was it that the trophy was enough? They were imposing horns, freshly removed from the carcass of a large musky beast, bred and kept in the farmer's field that these mountains had perversely felt like that day.

As I looked at the antlers, I was reminded of my own encounters with antlers and deer in the mountains, sometimes together, others apart. One time, when slightly off the beaten trod with Aidan, Munro-bagging in the Fannichs, I came across a single antler – ivory white against the green of the land and three-pronged, relatively small and perfectly formed. Walking a few steps back from Aidan at the time, I picked it up and gently prodded him from behind – teasing him to go faster. We looked in vain for the pair, knowing it would likely be a fruitless search. I don't know all that much about deer, but I doubt they shed both their antlers in exactly the same place and time. I strapped it to my rucksack; it's now my own trophy (although I feel more comfortable calling it a finding, a memento). It sits on a bookcase next to my painting easel at home in Otley, reminding me of higher places, the life within it and happy days in the mountains.

Another time I was running alone on some of the lesser-trodden hills of Mull, above and to the west of Craignure. As I began to descend a ridgeline in the mist, I suddenly found myself running within a herd. I must have unknowingly approached them downwind. Among these other animals my senses seemed heightened; I smelt and felt the warmth of their musk. They ran in different directions, no doubt surprised by the excursion of a human onto some of the quieter upland of Mull. On leaving the relative easy-going of the ridge to descend directly to the cottage we were staying in, I found the ground slow and tough. Thigh-deep heather and boggy groughs conspired to make it the roughest kind of descent. My legs got scratched to pieces; I was very mindful that this was the kind of place I could pick up dozens of ticks so I kept stopping to check. Generally steep, the gradient of the hillside eased off for a while, flattening to form a kind of small basin. It was here the deer had run to. I must have annoyed them as I approached them again, here was their hiding place, hidden from above and below by the curvature of the ground. They ran off again and I carried on my stumbling descent to reach the cottage.

It is that warm smell that most stays with me. For a few brief moments I was among them, running with these animals. Close enough to sense them with more than my eyes.

It seems wrong in my head that I went into Knoydart for a wilderness experience and left feeling that I had really just been to a big farm. Like the deer whose antlers were now strapped to the outside of the man's bag, I was controlled on the hillside, not free. Of course, the reasons I was controlled was so I would be 'safe' being kept to the main path up and down the mountain.

From up the top of Ladhar Bhienn I had also heard the incessant noise of some kind of machinery, carried on the wind from the edge of the peninsula. None of this fitted with my perceptions of how it would be. I love places like Knoydart so much and yet maybe it really is the romantic notion I carry for it that I love.

I am and was a typical tourist carrying an ideal about a place, who is disappointed when the reality of modern-day living encroaches as far as the most remote village on the UK mainland, despite the fact that in many ways these changes make the lives of those living in Inverie easier. This is not true for the whole of the Rough Bounds of Knoydart – travel north from Ladhar Beinn towards Barrisdale and Loch Hourn and it certainly begins to feel wilder. I suppose it should not be a surprise that the land closest to Inverie should be the most tamed.

There was an older man waiting at the quay for the ferry. Probably in his eighties, maybe he had lived his whole life in Inverie. As the boat arrived and the few foot passengers departed, before the crew let us passengers on they unloaded their cargo. The day's post, provisions – this ferry is the main transporter of all these things. The old guy smiled as he was passed a parcel from the boat, stamped large with the logo of Amazon Prime.

11. Quinaig
West

Aidan and the girls left me in the car park at the high point of the Ullapool road. Later we would meet at the end of my planned route, outside the Drumbeg Stores, on the coast road to Stoer. We were in Assynt again; it was late April. In among the toddler walks, bird-spotting and playing on the beaches, I was about to go for a snowy run in the hills.

The mountains were brooding. Summits wrapped in cloud, I could feel them more than see them. Snow flurries blew in the wind around my head, from the road I had more than 500 metres to climb to reach the summit I was heading for. I wondered what conditions would be like up there.

From this point in clear weather you can see Quinaig, Ben More Assynt, Conival, Canisp, Cul Mor, Suilven and more. These strange, beautiful hills, so old and worn that many stand alone, isolated and stark on the skyline.

I was set on climbing Quinaig. Not a hill itself but a range of three distinct summits – Spidean Coinich, Sàil Gharbh and Sàil Ghorm, meaning mossy peak, rough heel and blue heel respectively. The Gaelic name of this range is *A' Chuinneag* – the milk pail.

We had returned to stay on the coast at Stoer, from which Quinaig is the closest of the Assynt hills. Each morning I would look east to its imposing western face, a fortress of steep rock, set against whatever weather was blowing in. Quite distinct from one another, each of the three peaks of the Quinaig are pyramidal, the sails of a mountain.

From my starting point on the roadside at Quinaig's south-eastern end, I had in mind to run the three hills and then descend off its northern end, north-west from the summit of Sàil Ghorm. I would then turn to head south towards Loch an Leothaid, where I would meet a path that would take down Gleann Leireag to meet the road to Drumbeg. That was my plan anyway, but it started to feel more dubious as I gained height. The snow became deeper on the ground and was falling with increasing thickness.

I climbed Spidean Coinich first, following the path due west from the car park. As conditions worsened I pulled ski goggles from my rucksack, meaning I could see clearly, not having to squint against the snow blowing in my face. I already had all my warm and waterproof outer gear on and, should I need them, I had crampons in my pack and an axe strapped to it.

I reached the summit and then descended on a north-west bearing, taking care in the poor visibility to hold my line to be assured I'd not wander too close to the steep cliffs on the northern side of the mountain. In a while the descent eased off and I passed a little lochan. From the map I could see that the immediate risk from the descent in those conditions had passed. I felt relief, tempered by the knowledge that to go on meant I would likely experience a few more of these moments. While they are good as I enjoy the way they test my abilities to navigate and keep myself safe, they are wearying.

Visibility worsened again and the wind was getting stronger. I decided it would be better to descend than keep going. From the map I could see Bealach a Chornaidh, the col that separates

Sàil Gharbh from Spidean Coinich. It looked like it should be possible to descend west off the hill from there and that this was the last chance to do so before the steep crags on Quinaig's western face. The alternative was to retreat my steps until I was nearly back to the road and then contour around the hillside to meet the Tumlore to Nedd path. The latter was the safer option, but would have taken much longer. I was worried about soft snow on the steep ground immediately below the bealach, but also thought this would be short-lived.

After a little more consideration, I decided to descend from the bealach. I unstrapped the ice axe from the outside of my rucksack, looping its leash around my wrist. The snow was so soft that had I slipped there would have been no point in trying to arrest my fall with it, but it would be useful to push the shaft of the axe into the snow to gain an additional point of contact with the ground.

The snow had mostly accumulated in the widest parts of the shallow gully I was descending. Without it the terrain would have been steep grass, rock and scree. I stayed to the sides where the snow was less established, stepping my legs deeply into it, pushing down on the shaft of my ice axe to gain purchase on the ground below.

While I couldn't see the shape of the mountain due to the clag and snow, I imagined it from the map held in my hand. I'd studied it very closely the night before, in front of a roaring stove, back among the warmth of my family. Contours from the map lined my imaginary mountain, broken by the steep, dark crags to my right that now seemed menacing. Suddenly I felt very small and alone.

As my fears rose about avalanching myself off the mountain, it all started to feel very foolish. Why I did not accept the extra hour or so it would have taken by the safer option I do not know. I suppose part of me wanted to keep an element of challenge and adventure. If you are careless, misadventure lies just beyond; I was touching it and I knew it.

Having got to the point where I could see it was safer to keep descending rather than retrace my steps, I steadily and slowly made my way down with the snowline getting ever closer. I'd been correct in assuming the steep snowy ground would be relatively short-lived and I was nearing safer ground.

The snow became less deep and the going easier; eventually the land became more brown than white. That descent had been 'one of those' moments – something I shouldn't have done in the mountains, especially not alone. As I've got older I've experienced them far less and was annoyed, frustrated with myself that I had done it again. I could see my children's faces while I was up there.

I re-strapped my axe to my pack and set off at a run, over the bogland towards the track I would follow to Nedd. During all the nervous descending above I had dropped out of the cloud that was hanging around the higher ramparts of Quinaig. Now I had a view; the air was warmer. As I ran I looked out west, over the Assynt Levels.

I had been inspired to do this particular run over Quinaig and along to Drumbeg by the book I had been reading at the time. *Wild Voices* by Mike Cawthorne. A writer of the Highlands, within the book he recounts seven journeys, each of them inspired by other writers of the Highlands, among them Syd Scroggie, Neil Gunn, Rowena Farre. Cawthorne travelled around Ardnamurchan, followed the River Findhorn from its end where it flows into the Moray Firth and upstream to where it rises in the Monadhliath Mountains. He journeyed into Glen Affric, to Lewis, into the Cairngorms and explored Sutherland. In the chapter I was reading at the time, Cawthorne tells of traversing the Assynt Levels by canoe, a journey inspired in part by Norman MacCaig.

From my vantage point descending Quinaig, the Levels spread out below me. The land is undulating bogland and short rocky outcrops, interspaced with many lochans, on that day reflecting

the sky, grey with occasional glimpses of blue. I imagined
weaving a running or walking line across the ground, maybe
for a hot day when the occasional swim would prove to be both
enticing, and also the more direct line. While rough and slow
going underfoot, it is just the kind of ground I love to run across
– my favourite.

Nowadays this land is far more empty of the crofters who were
here in high numbers before the Clearances. Beyond the Levels,
on the coastline around Stoer and the handful of homes and the
land around them, I could also see signs of the new landowners,
the Assynt Crofters' Trust.

A few days before this I had gone with Aidan and the girls to look
out over the Levels from the south. Starting at Little Assynt, we
followed a footpath loop for a couple of miles. Our objective had
been to look for the pair of black-throated divers that had been
reported on Loch Beannach. Aidan had brought his telescope
along; he set it up at a high point on the track that looked over
the loch, and within ten minutes or so had it trained on the two
birds. We took turns to take a look. Their streamlined shape
suggested they would be great swimmers, as I took my turn to
watch one of them dived cleanly into the water.

I wondered whether Mike Cawthorne had seen these divers
when he paddled Loch Beannach as part of his three-day journey
across the Levels with his friend Clive and dog Holly. He does not
mention them; most likely the commotion of two people and a
dog in a canoe scared them away, even if they were there.

Always evocative of place and the mountains, Cawthorne's writing and his journeys have inspired my own through the years. His love for the Highlands shines through, the way he lyrically explores its history and culture, layering his own thoughts and experiences in with these, makes for exhilarating reading. The chapter telling of his paddle in Assynt exemplified this.

Assynt is a place for writers. During my first week-long visit in April 2011, I felt this; it made me want to be one too. At the time I was in the process of writing what would become my first book, piecing my thinking and stories together, seeking to learn more about what I was trying to convey through reading the words of others. During this trip from the bookshop in Ullapool, I brought and then devoured *At the Loch of the Green Corrie* by Andrew Greig.

This book is about a fishing trip Greig made to Assynt with friends at the behest of the dying Norman MacCaig who told him to go fishing 'at the loch of the green corrie' – Lochan a Choire Ghuirm. Greig's telling of this journey is also a beautiful exploration of himself, MacCaig, writing, ageing and friendship, all set against the Assynt landscape – a place of old mountains, of feelings of remoteness and of time that fires inspiration.

I have a lot to thank Greig for. In addition to his fine writing, he introduced me to Norman MacCaig and Kathleen Jamie. Reading his words also took me to Nan Shepherd and her masterpiece *The Living Mountain*.

MacCaig was something of a mentor to Greig, who introduced himself to MacCaig when he was a young poet still finding his way with words. Their friendship spanned decades. Imagine that – to have known MacCaig and spent time with him, to have heard his voice, smelled his pipe smoke, likely been on the receiving end of some sharp wit with kind intention. As I write these words, in my head I have MacCaig's poem 'Climbing Suilven'.

> Parishes dwindle. But my parish is
> This stone, this tuft, this stone
> And the cramped quarters of my flesh and bone.

In a few words MacCaig captures the atrocities of the Clearances, philosophises that the land is still its own, along with raising the small matters of religion and mortality, all with a backdrop of a glorious mountain. Imagine to have conversed with the man who wrote these words, to have talked about writing with him.

Continuing this daydream, I move on to meet Nan Shepherd, on a trod somewhere near the Shelter Stone, descending from the plateau, approaching the deep waters of Loch Avon, high in the Cairngorms. A warm summer's day with a light breeze, somewhere above us a skylark is singing. There are so many things I want to say, but instead say nothing at all. I have feelings of awe when I see her; we share a silent glance of greeting as we pass each other. Best not to disturb her thinking. Best to leave her to her beloved mountain.

Instead, separated by time, it is her words that take me there. I can go to the same places she went, see them for myself, listen for her voice echoing down the years. Mike Cawthorne understood this when he called them the 'wild voices'. These are people whose mountains are full of wildness and wonder, their words distil it and make them feel closer somehow.

After a mile or so of descending from the bealach on tussocks and bog I reached the track. An Old Way, a combination of grass, mud and rock, it skirts the north-eastern side of the Assynt Levels, slowly curving westwards, passing Loch an Leothaid to finish down Gleann Leireag and the road near Loch Nedd and its namesake township. The track was easier going underfoot; the weather continued to clear from the west. I looked out that way, to the sea. Glistening water, the sun still a while from the horizon, it was turning into a fine evening in Assynt.

For a while after passing the loch, the track follows the river that flows from it. The land changes from tundra to wooded glen. As the track finished and met the road I saw a few stags close by, their antlers looked fresh and pointed. They did not seem too timid; I slowed to a walk to take a longer look at them before they turned and left, jumping strongly over the ground and climbing back up onto the hill.

I love to cycle this road. It bends, rises and falls with the coastline. One way you can look out to sea, the other to Quinaig rising sharply upwards beyond the Assynt Levels. Following the road north-east takes you around the northern end of Quinaig to the road junction near Unapool and the impressive bridge over Loch Cairnbawn at Kylesku. From here you can look out over Loch Glendu and Loch Glencoul, the Stack of Glencoul and beyond, up onto the Ben More Assynt massif.

That evening I instead followed this curving road west. Having no wheels I ran the few miles to Drumbeg. My legs and feet made hard, repetitive movements along the tarmac; despite the lovely view I was reminded why I much prefer to run on the hill.

When I got there the store was closed. I sat down outside and waited for Aidan and the girls to arrive. Rather than relying on phone reception (more or less non-existent), we had agreed a time they would meet me, I was about an hour early, my run shortened by that early descent from Quinaig. Waiting on a bench in front of the stores, I pulled out the copy of *Wild Voices* from my rucksack and continued to read about Cawthorne's canoe journey, which just so happened to finish in Drumbeg. There was a funny kind of symmetry to it – there I was, sitting outside the place where I'd brought this book, reading about the author, his friend and dog, finishing their paddle close to the bench on which I was sitting.

When writing these words I remembered just how much I appreciated that waiting and reading time. I rarely stop still in places like that; I just don't seem to have the time. It was early evening, birdsong, fresh green and blossom on the trees, the place was full of new life. While it was winter on the mountain, spring was in the glen. All around me was that soft, clear kind of light you get in the west.

Epilogue

'O licht amo' the hills!'
Nan Shepherd

It is now summer. While the pandemic is still all around us, it is tempting to hope that the coming winter will not be so restricted and confined as the last.

Writing this book was soothing in these dark times. During lockdown the words poured out of me early in the morning and late at night, either side of the home-schooling and working hours. The sketches came too, as looking at my photos of these mountain journeys and my maps of this land led me to think further about their shape and their texture.

When I read through the book now I see a theme: this is a book about the west. As I wrote I found myself wondering why I was not writing of the Cairngorms. It's not that I love them any less than the places I have written of. The journeys over, around and through those hills, in winter and summer conditions, have been some of my finest.

I think I've worked it out.

For years now I have loved the work of Nan Shepherd. Of course, her classic and unique paean to the Cairngorms, *The Living Mountain*, but also her fiction and poetry. Within her only published poetry collection, *In the Cairngorms*, is a poem called 'Embodiment'.[14] Shepherd explores how the look and feel of the mountains, her beloved Grampians, are changed by the condition of light.

**There is no substance but light.
The visible worlds
Are light
Undergoing process of creation**

Since I read 'Embodiment', much like my experience of first seeing the Flowerdale Hills, these words have haunted me, inspired me. Nan Shepherd's words express the stark, inhuman wonders of the Cairngorms to such effect, although I wanted to tell my own Cairngorm mountain stories, I think I felt that trying to express them myself in words was not needed. I felt inhibited.

When I finished the first draft of this book, as often happens when I've spent a length of time writing intensely, my head turned to painting. This time with oils; it had been well over a year since I last painted on canvas. As I found myself doing this again, my style had changed. I'm suddenly all palette knives and texture rather than the smooth, blended strokes with brushes I had previously made. With this change in style has come a need to express the form and texture of mountains more boldly. I want to try to capture emotion and feeling as well as the scene itself.

When I got some new canvases and picked up a palette knife, to begin with I painted Lake District scenes. As I grew more confident and the desire to express my feelings grew, my head turned to the Cairngorms.

Instead of words, I think my mountain stories of these hills are going to be expressed through painting. At the moment it feels like it's going to be a series based on photographs of three journeys I have made into the Cairngorms, two in midwinter, the other in midsummer.

At the time of writing I have painted three of these scenes.

The first is of the Pools of Dee, looking to the south from the high-point of the Lairig Ghru, that renowned highway that connects

Deeside and Speyside, cutting deeply through the Cairngorm Plateau. It shows the early River Dee, just beginning to flow amongst the pinky-grey granite scree that lines this high pass, the greens and darker greys of the steep grass and craggy gound that swoops down to this bealach, on one side from Braeriach, the other Ben Macdui. South beyond the immediacy of the Pools of Dee, two mountain profiles rise up – Cairn Toul and Bod am Deamhaim (or Devil's Point), greyed and blurred by the heavy rain of an incoming front. This memory is from late June 2019 when, after three days of good weather running about exploring these mountains, I could see I was going to get very wet.

The second and third are two scenes looking to different places from the same vantage point on Ben Avon at the eastern end of the Cairngorm plateau.

One looks to the north-west, over the ridges, peaks and granite tors of Stob an t'Sluichd, Creag Mhòr and Bynack More. Stob an t'Sluichd in the foreground is a golden yellow in the light. The hills behind are dark, graduated in their blueness. Nan Shepherd writes of this blue and so too does Rebecca Solnit – it is Solnit's 'blue of distance', the blue we can never reach.[15]

The third scene looks towards the summit tor of Leabaidh an Daimh Bhuidhe. The heavy grey cloud behind this top makes it appear bright, the land around it coloured by granite boulders and the muted green artic tundra. With my palette knife I tried to capture the shape of the tor and its place rising from the plateau. This flat landscape fascinates me. With the exception of Ben Nevis, the highest mountains in the land rise up out of it, but it is really one mountain, worn away through the epochs to the rounded peaks and depressions that we see and feel today.

These paintings don't reproduce well in black and white. If you would like to see them I have put them on my website, and will add more paintings to this page as I go.[16]

Nan was right – it is all about light. I will keep looking and trying to capture it on canvas, re-exploring the Cairngorms from a distance, remembering being amongst them. Hopefully, soon enough, I will be back there. More than anything I want to gaze into the depths of Loch Avon, feel the fearful infinite that Nan describes in *The Living Mountain*. After that I think I will try to paint that feeling – impossible perhaps, but surely something worth attempting.

Otley,
July 2021

Acknowledgements

I wrote this book during a time that was hard for many of us. My family helped me, as did meeting with my friends – MJ, Sarah and Kate – for walks, runs and bike rides on the Otley Chevin and Ilkley Moor.

It feels strange to write this, but the world of social media was also a place where I found release – in particular through other artists and writers sharing their work. John Altringham's watercolours of north-west Scotland, Jenny McLaren's paintings of skies, birds and mountains on old maps and Mark Goodwin's tweeted poems are three examples – there are many more. Thank you for sharing!

Thank you as ever to Jo Allen and Rhiannon Hughes for all they do making Little Peak books with such enthusiasm and commitment.

Many thanks to Lucy Wallace for writing such a lovely foreword – hopefully one day we will meet and have a wander over Arran's wonderful mountains together.

Thank you also to Andrea Priestley, Helen Mort, David Lintern, Alex Roddie, Geoff Cox, Rich Seipp, Tim Woods and Faye Latham, and to my family – Aidan, Alanna and Robyn.

Biography

Heather Dawe is a writer, painter, runner, cyclist and climber. She works in data innovation and lives in Otley, Yorkshire, with her partner and young family.

Her books include *Traceless*, *Adventures in Mind* and *A Cycling Year*; she has written for print and online publications, including *The Guardian*.

Heather was an editor of *Waymaking*, which won the 2019 Banff Mountain Literature Award. She was on the jury for the 2021 Banff Mountain Literature Competition.

Finding inspiration for her writing and painting during the time she spends in the mountains and her local fells and dales, Heather increasingly shares adventures in the hills with her young daughters as they grow.

See Heather's artwork and writing at **www.heatherdawe.co.uk**, on Twitter **@heatherldawe** and Instagram **@heatherdawe**

Bibliography: references and further reading

[1] MacCaig, Norman 'A Man In Assynt', from *The Collected Poems of Norman MacCaig*, edited by Ewen McCaig, (Polygon, 2005)

[2] Tim Robinson's maps: https://digital.library.nuigalway.ie/islandora/object/nuigalway%3Arobinson-maps?display=list

[3] Robinson, Tim, *Connemara: Listening to the Wind*, (Penguin Books, 2007)

[4] Jenny McLaren's Instagram: https://www.instagram.com/jennymclarenart/

[5] Ross, Anne, *Folklore of the Scottish Highlands*, (Tempus, 2000)

[6] Maclean, Sorley, 'An Cuilithionn 1939' from *The Cuillin 1939 and Unpublished Poems*, edited by Christopher Whyte, (Association for Scottish Literature Studies, 2011)

[7] Maclean, Sorley, 'Hallaig' from *Hallaig and Other Poems*, introduced by Angus Peter Campbell and Aonghas MacNeacail, (Polygon, 2014)

[8] Maxell, Gavin, *Ring of Bright Water*, (Unicorn Press, 2014)

[9] Abbey, Edward, *Desert Solitaire*, (The University of Arizona Press, 1988)

[10] Cawthorne, Mike, *Wild Voices: Journeys Through Time in the Scottish Highlands*, (Birlinn, 2014)

[11] Grieg, Andrew, *At the Loch of the Green Corrie*, (Quercus, 2010)

[12] Shepherd, Nan, *The Living Mountain*, (Canongate, 2008)

[13] MacCaig, Norman 'Climbing Suilven' from *The Collected Poems of Norman MacCaig*, edited by Ewen McCaig, (Polygon, 2005)

[14] Shepherd, Nan, 'Embodiment' from *In the Cairngorms*, foreword by Robert Macfarlane, (Galileo Publishers, 2014)

[15] Solnit, Rebecca, *A Field Guide to Getting Lost*, (Canongate, 2005)

[16] www.heatherdawe.co.uk/cairngormslight

Excerpts from Norman MacCaig's *The Many Days* reproduced by kind permission of Berlinn Limited.

Excerpts from Nan Shepherd's poetry from *In the Cairngorms* reproduced by kind permission Galileo Publishers, Cambridge.

Lightning Source UK Ltd.
Milton Keynes UK
UKHW021530061021
391728UK00004B/204